Wooden Spoon

Rugby's charity supporting disadvantaged children and young people

RUGBYWORLD
Yearbook 2008

Editor

Ian Robertson

Photographs

Getty Images

GreenUmbrella
Publishing

This book has been produced for Green Umbrella Publishing
by Lennard Books
a division of Lennard Associates Ltd
Windmill Cottage
Mackerye End
Harpenden
Herts AL5 5DR

This edition first published in the UK in 2007
by Green Umbrella Publishing

www.greenumbrella.co.uk

Paperback   ISBN 978 1 906229 16 0
Hardback   ISBN 978 1 906229 48 1

Production Editor: Chris Marshall
Design Consultant: Paul Cooper
Jacket Design: Kevin Gardner
Printed and bound in Slovenia

The publishers would like to thank Getty Images for providing most of the photographs for this book. The publishers would also like to thank Fotosport UK, Inphopics, Chris Thau and Wooden Spoon for additional material. The photograph of Scott Quinnell on page 10 is reproduced courtesy of www.Kasstzam.com and that of Kyran Bracken on page 13 courtesy of Nicky Johnson/ITV plc.

A la recherche du temps perdu

Contents

OFFICIAL
BEER

ENGLAND
RUGBY

Greene King IPA
Britain's favourite cask beer

GREENE KING
IPA
nothing to prove

FOREWORD

by HRH THE PRINCESS ROYAL

BUCKINGHAM PALACE

HRH The Princess Royal,
Royal Patron of Wooden Spoon,
opens a Spoon project in Exeter.

The publication of the Wooden Spoon Rugby Annual is always a time to reflect upon the work of the charity in the previous year. I recall that, when I became Patron of Wooden Spoon in 1996 the charity was at the start of a long journey to develop a regional structure throughout the UK and Ireland.

Today, Wooden Spoon has 44 Regions from Aberdeen to Guernsey and from Suffolk to Belfast. In the past twelve months, these Regions have raised a record £1m for their work with disadvantaged children. These are not paid staff but volunteers giving their energies and expertise to the charity in a most demonstrable way. I commend their efforts to the readers of this year's Annual.

The past twelve months was a record year for the charity as a whole. The extra funds available enabled the Trustees of Wooden Spoon to support more disadvantaged children and young people than ever before. In the mid-90s, five or six projects a year were accomplished. This past 12 months saw Wooden Spoon support 46 projects. Working within hospitals, schools and the broader charity sector Wooden Spoon helps children and young people who are disadvantaged physically, mentally or socially. Perhaps as importantly, they are seen as real partners by those entrusted with your funding.

The formula of a small central team supported by hundreds of volunteers and over 10,000 social members is one that clearly works for Wooden Spoon. Next year, the charity celebrates its 25th Anniversary, what can you do to help?

Anne

Wooden Spoon

Rugby's charity supporting disadvantaged children and young people

I Don't Want an Office Job!

by JULIAN CRABTREE

Royal Patron: HRH The Princess Royal
Patrons: Rugby Football Union • Scottish Rugby Union
                 Welsh Rugby Union • Irish Rugby Football Union

*R*etiring is hard enough at the best of times, but for professional rugby players who still have their best years ahead of them, life after rugby can be a very scary proposition. WOODEN SPOON finds out why the transformation may not be as frightening as they think and why their skills are highly desirable.

When Brendan Cannon was asked what front-row skills could be applied in business, the former Wallaby hooker replied: 'Well if you don't get the results you want, you just grab the guy and you head butt him. You always manage to get the result in the end.'

While many an employer may well frown over these tactics, players who are looking towards a life after rugby certainly do have plenty of skills that can be transferred to the business world. Companies looking for prospective employees recognise that the DNA that makes up professional and elite sportspeople is very desirable. They are highly driven, very ambitious, results-orientated and high-achieving individuals. If you look at any job specification in any sector, that is exactly what they are looking for.

Despite professional rugby still being in its infancy, we are seeing players retiring from the game who have known nothing but rugby their whole working life. This can be extremely stressful – not only giving up all you have known but also finding the right profession once the curtain comes down on your rugby career. However, companies buy into the skills of rugby players and realise that what they lack – which would be skills and experience in that industry – can be easily rectified by in-house training and support.

Former England winger Jon Sleightholme knows the stress involved with retiring and was determined to make his own way in the business world. His knowledge of what it takes to be equally successful on the field and in the boardroom saw him become one of the founding directors of Careers After Sport, which has been going for just over three years.

'The challenge that a lot of players face is finding something to replace rugby with,' said Sleightholme. 'A lot of players will have opportunities with plenty of people wanting to give them a chance, particularly if they have a high profile in the game.

'Doors do open up for you and the challenge is deciding which door to walk through.

'Sometimes the offers are not totally genuine and more importantly, is it the right thing for you to get involved with?'

All sportspeople, not only professional rugby players, have committed 10-15 years or more to a certain way of life that has dictated everything that they have done. In a way you could say that they have been blinkered, and when those blinkers finally come off the challenge is how they will replace the buzz of playing and winning.

'Rugby players have a strong team ethic and know how to work with

BELOW Jon Sleightholme in his pomp at Bath shows Jason Robinson, then of Wigan, a clean pair of heels in the clash of the codes match at Twickenham in 1996.

FACING PAGE Matt Dawson, one of the busiest former rugby stars, made a dream come true for Michael Heazelton, after a serious brain operation, when he introduced him to the whole England team at Cardiff.

LEFT Scott Quinnell opens a new sensory room for special needs children on behalf of Wooden Spoon at Doubletrees School in St Blazey, near Par, Cornwall.

BELOW Glory days. Scott Quinnell celebrates scoring for the British & Irish Lions in the first Test against Australia at Brisbane in 2001. The No. 8 started in all three Tests on the tour, to add to his 52 caps for Wales.

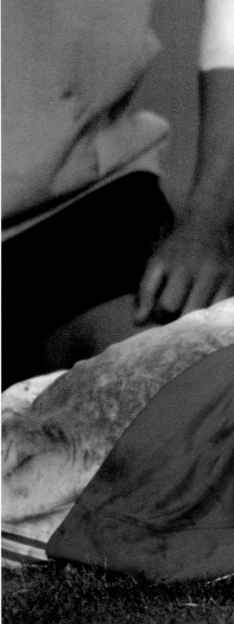

others towards the same goal, and while that may not be as exciting as on the field, they can still get a buzz from being successful,' said Sleightholme, who won 12 caps for England.

One player who has grasped retirement with both hands is Scott Quinnell. Quinnell always planned to retire at the end of the 2004-05 season, and although a hand injury forced him to give up a few weeks early, he was prepared for the next chapter of his life.

Belonging to one of the most famous rugby families in the world, Quinnell had a unique insight into life after the oval ball. Not only did he watch his father play international rugby while running a successful business, but he also experienced the transformation from being an amateur player to being a professional one.

'When I first started playing I used to work nine to five, train a couple of days a week and play on the weekends,' said Quinnell.

'By the time I retired, all the players were professional and rugby was our only job.

'We are seeing the first generation of professional rugby players starting to retire who have only ever known rugby, that can be difficult not having done anything else before.

'I was quite lucky as I was doing some work in the media while I was still playing rugby. I was doing some work with Sky Sports and doing a column in the paper, so when it came to retiring I knew I could carry on doing that.'

Sleightholme agrees with Quinnell that it is harder for the modern-day rugby player.

'My generation knew what they wanted to do because they had done it before. It is difficult for the guys today, there is a real fear factor about life after rugby.

'But it does not have to be a frightening thing at all, if they take control of it and address it, things are not as scary as they first seem.'

Sleightholme and Quinnell also agree that the earlier you start looking to the future the better, but trying to tell a 20-year-old who is just starting out to think about life after the game is easier said than done. 'Let's be honest, when you are in your early twenties you think you are indestructible and you are not even thinking about the end of your career,' explained Sleightholme.

'But one of the most important things to understand is that while you are playing professional rugby, you are in the limelight.

'You need to get an understanding of how to network yourself around the business and the corporate partners involved in the club and to build a network of contacts to help you once you have retired.'

The high profile earned by players can also benefit charities, something which is very close to Quinnell's heart. 'I do a lot of work for charities like Wooden Spoon and various charities around the country,' said Quinnell.

Retirement can also bring about a transformation in other parts of life, and with his media career gaining momentum, Quinnell was forced to face his demons. Despite his many battles on the field

ABOVE Spoon ambassador Gavin Hastings tries a new line in table tennis kit at the opening of a new suite of rooms for the volunteer charity Bfriends at Craigmillar in Edinburgh. His playing partner is project worker Olivia Beddard.

FACING PAGE Former England scrum half Kyran Bracken found post-rugby fame in the ITV show *Dancing on Ice,* which he won with Melanie Lambert.

with the likes of Lawrence Dallaglio, Quinnell's greatest challenge came after he retired and he took on his dyslexia in typical Quinnell fashion – head on. Quinnell started out on a non-invasive and drug-free programme called DORE, which is a controversial exercise treatment that claims to cure dyslexia by directly addressing the physiological source of the problem. The science behind this programme is basically that exercise stimulates the cerebellum and allows the processing of information more rapidly.

'A year after my retirement I was lucky enough to be able to do the DORE programme and challenge myself that way,' explained Quinnell.

'It was a different challenge, a much more personal one and I did a documentary on dyslexia with the BBC which made a lot more people aware of dyslexia.'

Quinnell's rugby profile, and his honesty and bravery in facing his problem, was the perfect vehicle to bring dyslexia into the public eye. However, while the likes of Quinnell, Jason Leonard, Gavin Hastings and Martin Johnson have profiles that will always be linked with rugby, there is the danger that some players may not have the same public longevity.

'Without a doubt employing a high-profile sportsman or -woman certainly has its benefits on many levels,' explained Sleightholme. 'From a PR profile to working on corporate and social responsibility. However, we try wherever possible to build a working strategy for a sportsman so he has some very tangible and measurable skills and goals.

'They don't want to be performing monkeys for the rest of their lives.'

Living off past glories is not an option for most sportsmen and -women. They want to be recognised for more than what they did on the pitch.

'They want to be as successful as they can in their next career,' added Sleightholme.

'Obviously there is an angle to the shaking hands and taking photos which is great, but a sportsman's profile only lasts so long.

'They want to have a bit more meat to their career bones than that, a little more depth.'

Rugby clubs are well aware of their responsibility to guide and develop their players' skills – on and off the field.

Most top-flight academies have initiatives to prepare their young players for life beyond professional rugby. Obviously their aim is to develop the rugby skills that will benefit the club. However, there is also the support and guidance to achieve qualifications and experience necessary for when the playing days are over.

The Professional Rugby Players' Association (PRA), which represents the interests of professional players in England, is also highly committed to preparing its members for life after rugby. The organisation currently has three Player Development Managers working with the Guinness Premiership clubs in areas such as improving study skills, developing business ideas and exploring future career options.

Exploring future career options is key, especially when the most used phrase that Sleightholme hears is 'I don't want an office job'. It makes sense that having spent the last ten years getting into the best possible shape, the last thing you want is to be tied to a desk.

However, with today's technology, that is not really an issue. Companies are more flexible and more people work from home. In the Internet age you can be very flexible.

Another misconception that Sleightholme faces from young players is the rose-tinted view about what the business sector is all about. Finance has been the traditional pathway for rugby players to take. But there are a lot more choices available these days.

Rugby players have earned a reasonable salary while playing and they want to replicate that in the outside world. That is easier said than done, especially when they don't have a lot of experience. Because of this a lot of them gravitate to sales and business development within different sectors because there are opportunities to be earning a good salary fairly quickly.

'If they want to earn a particular amount, then that obviously narrows down the sector they can work in,' said Sleightholme.

'We certainly try and broaden their horizons and make them look at their strengths and what sort of working environment they will develop in.'

They may not have the skills yet, but companies spend a fortune sending their employees on courses to learn what rugby players have got in abundance. Sleightholme's advice is don't panic. There are plenty of opportunities out there; the challenge is finding the one that is right for you.

One man who has explored a different route after putting his rugby career on ice is Kyran Bracken. Despite being trained as a lawyer, Bracken has established himself on the public-speaking circuit, where he not only successfully promotes himself but also Wooden Spoon.

Bracken retired from rugby having won 51 caps for England, including three as captain, but was soon back in the public eye when he appeared in the show *Dancing on Ice*. The programme soon became one of the most successful reality TV shows and after three months of extreme training, Bracken and his ice-skating partner Melanie Lambert were crowned champions.

Bracken showed not only his commitment to Spoon but also his generosity by donating his appearance fee and his winner's bonus – after treating his family to a well-deserved holiday for putting up with him during the show.

By broadening his career in the public-speaking world, Bracken has become a great ambassador for Spoon and embodies not only the ethos of the charity but also how one can keep on winning and succeeding long after the boots have been hung up.

COMMENT
& FEATURES

Semper Bonus Homo Tiro Est

by PAUL STEPHENS

'The global enterprise, which for decades relied upon its membership of an international fraternity for mutual help and fellowship, has been corrupted in the last few years'

There are those who believe the notion that the transition to professionalism in rugby union, one of the world's oldest team games, would be tranquil and a model of reposeful and undisturbed calm. It was not just wishful thinking, but bunkum, not far short of a national misadventure; and those who relied on its credence had little or no appreciation of the consequences. What we have now is a combustible mix of sulphur and adrenalin, despite the fact that attendances at Guinness Premiership matches and Heineken Cup games have shown a welcome increase.

The global enterprise, which for decades relied upon its membership of an international fraternity for mutual help and fellowship, has been corrupted in the last few years. There is altogether an absence of the qualities of scholarly rigour, careful argument and clear-headed judgment. This has given way to eccentric deceit, unscrupulousness, turpitude and lies, which debases the game at the summit. Unless the very best players and coaches are being paid the full amount, they will soon be off and away, to be replaced by players and coaches from overseas, many of whom are of doubtful skill and nearing the end of their careers.

John Brain was director of rugby at Worcester, and though he saved them from relegation at the end of last season, he was soon shown the exit door by Cecil Duckworth, to be replaced by Mike Ruddock and Clive Griffiths. Ruddock wanted Griffiths at Sixways, and when asked why he changed clubs from Doncaster to Worcester, Griffiths' reply was: 'It was Money'. Not much room for quirky sentiment or loyalty there. His departure from Castle Park, despite having a year left on his contract, was not without rancour.

'We have a situation where someone has left with 12 months to run on a two-year contract,' said Doncaster chairman Steve Lloyd. 'We have not made any decisions, but we have to carry out our duties as directors.' Could this be wishful thinking?

Griffiths did a tidy if unspectacular job at Castle Park, taking the club to third in National One, though they failed to beat Leeds and were unable to make their mark in the promotion race.

Brain meantime has found some solace, having been recruited by Bristol as their forwards coach. Martin Haag, who was in the job for the preceding three years and had a contract not due to expire until 2008, has been axed, so Brain will appear at the Memorial Ground this season. The merry-go-round of players and coaches does not end there, but has gathered impressive momentum.

At Worcester, New Zealand winger Rico Gear has signed on. He follows fellow All Blacks Sam Tuitupou and Greg Rawlinson, Fiji international Netani Talei and Samoan full back Loki Crichton, all new arrivals at Sixways since the end of last season. Northampton are no strangers to the recruitment of overseas players and coaches, with Bruce Reihana, Mark Robinson, Sam Harding and Carlos Spencer, all from New Zealand, as well as many others ineligible to play for England, like the South African flanker Joe van Niekerk, who has signed a three-year contract. At Newcastle, Carl

ABOVE Former Bath lock Martin Haag, who was contracted to Bristol until 2008, found himself replaced as forwards coach at the Memorial Ground by ex-Worcester boss John Brain.

FACING PAGE South African back-row forward Joe van Niekerk, here tackled by Mils Muliaina, has joined the 'foreign legion' of overseas players in English rugby.

Hayman was recently recruited to join Joe McDonnell in the Falcons front row. What a combination. The Scot Ross Beattie, who will be 30 in November, returns to Kingston Park after spells with Bristol, Northampton, Border Reivers and Newport Gwent Dragons. Do you need to know more to understand that the game in England is being taken over by foreigners, or is this enough?

Gianfranco Zola, a sparkling diamond when he was at Stamford Bridge, was adamant at the European Under 21 football competition in Arnhem recently, when he talked specifically of the need for the Premiership to introduce a quota on foreign players to assist England. Advising the nation on the need to cut back on imports may sound strange from a Sardinian voted Footballer of the Year, but Zola was always more missionary than mercenary. It pains him to see England struggle. 'Bringing in too many foreign players is not always the right thing to do,' says Zola. But do the Premiership managers or the owners care? Not a bit; and it could soon be like this in rugby union.

There is so much money washing about in the England game that the blazers have lost sight of the demise of Orrell and Wakefield. Does it matter? So long as rugby union in England is thriving, why worry? At the very top it is in predictably good shape, but further down there are signs of waning interest. Does a young player really want to be sucked into a game that has as its main absorption the enrolment of extrinsic players who have no feel for the clubs they join and who sign only for the cash? Within ten years the game of rugby union will not be as it is now. It will be like rugby league, heaven help us.

Scotland is without rugby league, but what a mess the union game is in that country. The SRU is in exigent debt, so much so that it has disbanded the Borders. Glasgow and Edinburgh and the national side remain. At Murrayfield they get only nominal crowds. Many of their players are now with clubs elsewhere, and neither of their two remaining districts has won the Heineken Cup. Down in the Borders at Gala, Hawick and Melrose there is despair: they have seen their beloved game taken from them and almost destroyed. The late Gordon Brown would spin in his grave.

With the possible exception of Llanelli, not much is happening in Wales, which used to be a gem in the bejewelled crown. But at least they can put out a decent international team and fill the Millennium Stadium, though winning the Heineken Cup is beyond any of their clubs. Given that rugby union is something of a religion in Wales, the game promises to remain in good heart for at least the next few years; for how long thereafter, remains to be seen. The rich are getting richer and the strong stronger.

What of Ireland? They have their strongest national side for many years and two Heineken Cup wins – for Ulster in 1999, when clubs from England took no part, and for Munster, who were triumphant in 2006 – but they always thought that they could have won more. The blazing Heineken row that featured the daunting Doctor Syd Millar, chairman of the International Rugby Board, was settled finally, with Mark McCafferty, the chief executive of Premier Rugby, saying: 'Some of [Millar's] comments and observations are wildly inaccurate and alas reflect the lack of general understanding of the issues at stake.' Francis Baron, the RFU's chief executive, said: 'The big issue is money.'

This brings me to refereeing. In more than 20 years of writing match reports for the national newspapers, I have castigated the referee only three times. The first was a long time ago. The second came at Northampton, in action against Leeds at Franklin's Gardens in the Premiership in January 2005. Steve Leyshon was blindingly lenient and I said so. He was never given another Premiership game.

Two years later at Edgeley Park, Sale met Ospreys in the Heineken Cup. A record crowd were incensed by Alain Rolland's incompetence. The Ospreys were lying on the ball, continually offside, interfering with play and deliberately obstructive. Later in the game, the Ospreys flanker Mike Powell lay motionless for fully six minutes in the lee of the far stand. The Ospreys faithful – mostly grouped in that area – were shouting at the touch judge, who did nothing. Neither did Mr Rolland. It was a masterful display of unfitted and maladroit administration.

In my report I said that if the Heineken Cup authorities nominated him for another fixture, they too should be called to book. A copy of my report, with a covering letter, was sent to Derek McGrath of ERC in Dublin, by international mail, which required a signature. He must

FACING PAGE Carl Hayman, who has joined Newcastle Falcons, salutes the crowd at Carisbrook after his final Super 14 match for the Highlanders in May.

have received it. I received no reply. After all, I am only a journalist. It beggars belief that some do not criticise referees, though are only too aware of the need to carp at the indifferent performance of the players.

Geoffrey Thompson, the quiet man from Sheffield, is now a member of the FIFA executive committee, and has been elevated to the position of the most influential man produced by British football since Sir Stanley Rous. Thompson is the former general manager and company secretary of Doncaster Rovers. His role as chairman of the Football Association has brought criticism for the perceived lack of leadership and a failure to act on key issues like quotas for non-English-qualified players in the Premiership. Where have we heard that one before?

The RFU, under the stewardship of Francis Baron, have become money obsessed, though it must be said that they are in a much better position than many other countries, despite overlooking the influx of overseas players, which threatens disruption, disorder and tumult in the game. In Ireland, the redevelopment of Lansdowne Road has taken much of the IRFU's resources; it can only take time before the funding of Munster, Leinster and Ulster is called into question. What then?

Let us, however, not question Martial's Latin dictum: *Semper Bonus Homo Tiro Est*. A good man is always a novice in the ways of the world.

FACING PAGE TOP Alain Rolland takes charge in the Heineken Cup semi-final between Leicester Tigers and Llanelli Scarlets at the Walkers Stadium in April.

FACING PAGE BOTTOM Sébastien Chabal and Brent Cockbain fall out during January's Heineken Cup match between Sale and the Ospreys at Edgeley Park.

BELOW Demolition begins as Lansdowne Road is converted into a 50,000-seater venue.

Official Assistance
the Rise of the TMO

by STEPHEN JONES

'Sometimes mauls collapse in a heap over the line, and there is no way that any one of 67 camera angles can reveal whether or not the touchdown has been made'

Gradually, in sport after sport, the idea that the main official's word is law is being eroded, and thank goodness for that. The man in the middle, the man in the umpire's chair, the man in the umpire's white coat, the referee, the man with the whistle – whoever the man in authority is, he now has help in making his decisions. Technological help.

At Wimbledon this year we had the first official use of Hawkeye, to adjudicate on some of the contested line calls. God knows if it was actually accurate, but it was cool, exciting, it looked great and it did at least seem to be a solid guide; in cricket, in some one-day events in 2007, we had technology officially ruling on lbw decisions as well as run-outs and catches, rather than just providing a guide for followers and the television audience as to whether the batsman might, or might not, have been out. Cricket may even bite the bullet and make almost every decision a mechanical one.

BELOW Touchdown or not? The TMO ruled that the ball had been held up and so disallowed this try by France against Italy in Paris in 2006.

The use of technology is increasing; key calls are being taken out of the hands of the main official. And as a result, many more are being made correctly. There are some minor problems. Calls being challenged in American football and rugby league can take ages for the adjudication, though if there is a decent screen to show the replays, then at least a modicum of tension can grow. But sport is now so good, so moneyed, so important that surely the officials themselves are wholeheartedly in favour of the principle that they can avoid looking like total prats.

In rugby, the Television Match Official (TMO) has generally been a good thing. Nevertheless, the system is inequitable since only those games being adequately covered by television can provide a satisfactory range of cameras for a proper TMO decision. And there is another problem – the vexed question of the grounding of the ball under driving mauls.

Sometimes mauls collapse in a heap over the line, and there is no way that any one of 67 camera angles can reveal whether or not the touchdown has been made. In such cases the TMO is guessing just as much as the referee in the first place and so cannot award a try. I remember Andre Watson, a South African referee acting as TMO, awarding South Africa a try against England in 2001 which not one single camera angle even hinted might have been scored.

What needs to happen is that the referee must be allowed to use his experience to judge, if the cameras cannot. I remember Argentina being robbed of a try against Australia in the early years of the TMO when about 14 Puma forwards drove over the line together, crashed in a heap around the ball in the company of one tangential Aussie who was nowhere near the ball, and because no camera angle actually caught the blindingly obvious fair try, then no try was awarded.

Yet at least the concept of a player being awarded a try in the corner when he actually curved out into the sixth row of the stand is a thing of the past. Although effectively the use of the TMO is restricted to rulings on the touchdown itself, on the grounding and whether the ball carrier

> **BELOW** Was he in touch? After reviewing all the evidence, the TMO ruled that Jonny Wilkinson had scored a legitimate try against Scotland at Twickenham.

went into touch-in-goal or hit the corner flag before touching down, it can still avoid horrible errors at the sharp end of the field.

How far can we go? Is the TMO already having too much of a say? Certainly not. We must never be afraid of technology and always be afraid of horrible decisions affecting massive matches. So I am delighted to hear that the International Rugby Board are actively considering extending the use of the TMO.

The guiding light behind many of the improvements in refereeing in the past two seasons is Paddy O'Brien, the amiable, clever and rather forceful Kiwi who is the refereeing manager of the IRB. O'Brien has done excellent work in improving the standard of the elite Test referees, and recently, after decades in which southern hemisphere referees were always given the vast majority of the top Tests, O'Brien presided over a selection process for Rugby World Cup 2007, which has seven European referees and only five from the southern hemisphere.

Good on O'Brien for righting the wrongs of the years, though it is also arguable that the southern hemisphere deserves only two places on that 12-man panel; but that, for now, is another story.

Our Paddy has extended the use of the TMO in a clever way. He insists that referees now demand of the TMO any evidence that they *cannot* award a try. The Pumas would have been allowed their try against Australia because there was no reason not to give it, rather than having it disallowed because there was no actual evidence in favour of it.

But O'Brien is now engaged in a consultative process with the major rugby countries with a view to extending the use of the TMO so that he can adjudicate in areas of the field other than the in-goal. There is a proposed law change that the corner flag is moved back out of the way so that tries can be scored in the corner provided that there is no grounding of the carrier over the sideline. Until now, to touch the flag before the touchdown has ruled out the try.

Further, O'Brien and the IRB are actively considering whether the unfairness of missed knock-ons could be erased by allowing the TMO to rewind and look for such offences. The thinking is that

this procedure could only be used in the very move leading to a try. Knock-ons in other indeterminate moves would not be examined, but if the alleged offence took place in a move which, even after several phases, ended in a try, then any part of the move could be examined, no matter if it took place 80 yards from the try line. There are several other areas when the TMO might also be allowed into the game.

There is still much to work out before any of this becomes law. O'Brien would not for the moment consider having forward passes decided with reference to the TMO, even if the move ended in a score. Shame. Referees these days stand idly by and allow an absolutely roaring torrent of forward passes, especially in the inside backs positions behind the scrum.

Frankly, I would even consider allowing the TMO to rule on forward passes. O'Brien's reservation is that cameras angles would often be unable to give us an accurate picture. But in these days when all pitches are beautifully manicured, there are any number of white lines or lines made by the mowing machines marching across the pitch at right angles to the touch line. Rugby league has found it easy to spot forward passes on the playback and, using the same informal grid of white lines and mowing lines, to judge if chasing runners were in front of the ball when it was kicked.

You must not go too far. You cannot hold up matches ten times per half. There have to be strong protocols. The technology available has to be of high class and the TMO has to be an expert twiddler of the knobs. We cannot all be expected to hang around talking about the weather through interminable delays. But sport is moving into an era in which the sanctity of the official's decision has been replaced by a demand for the correct decisions to be made. If technology can keep disputes and rank bad calls to a minimum, then it is silly not to plug it in.

The Birth of the Cup
the Men Who Changed Rugby

by **CHRIS THAU**

'Arguably this was one of the most significant votes in the history of the IRB, which, born in 1886, was just one year short of its centenary'

On 20 March 1985, at the International Rugby Board meeting in Paris, a momentous vote was taken at the end of a marathon four-hour session. The then chairman of the board (at the time the IRB was chaired in rotation by the member unions), Australia's long-serving international administrator Dr Roger Vanderfield, put to a ballot the following motion: 'The Board considered the feasibility study entitled "World Cup Rugby" … and resolved to accept the principle of an International Tournament as outlined … but subject to it being under the control of the International Board'. The wording of the motion, which clearly stipulated the holding of one tournament only, was important, as the opposition to it was very strong, and even some of those who had supported it had strong doubts about the adverse effect a rugby world cup would have on the fabric of the game. Arguably this was one of the most significant votes in the history of the IRB, which, born in 1886, was just one year short of its centenary.

The room was filled with some of the most distinguished administrators the game has ever had. Alongside Vanderfield sat the other Australian representative, Ross Turnbull, a former Wallaby who played a significant role in the launch of the tournament. New Zealand, who had been working closely with Australia to produce the feasibility study that was debated at the meeting, were represented by former All Black captain and coach Bob Stuart and Ces Blazey, arguably one of New Zealand's finest administrators. England had two very distinguished former internationals in former captain John Kendall-Carpenter and Albert Agar, while the Irish representatives were former Lions and Ireland captain and coach Ronnie Dawson and Harry McKibbin, a war hero and former Irish international. Keith Rowlands, a former Wales and Lions lock forward, and Gwylim Treharne, a leading administrator and future Welsh Rugby Union president, were there on behalf of the WRU. South Africa's delegates were Dr Danie Craven, the world's best known rugby personality, and his lifelong friend and colleague Dr Fritz Eloff, the world's leading expert on Kalahari lions. The French Federation, the hosts of the meeting, had their long-standing president Albert Ferrasse and André Bosc, a senior SNCF administrator, as their board representatives, while Scotland had two of their leading administrators, Bill Connon and George Burrell, the latter a former Scottish international and referee. Tension was in the air as the then honorary secretary of the board, John Hart, himself a former Scotland international, announced the beginning of the session.

Dr Vanderfield takes up the story. 'It was the second day of the meeting and we had gone through the preliminaries all day. We discussed the feasibility study produced by ARU and NZRU as well as all aspects and issues, this and that. Two aspects came up strongly during the debate, one was the financial argument, with the majority convinced that we could not make a profit, and the second, and equally significant, was the concern that an RWC would lead to professionalism, which of course it did.

'As the day wore on, I kept making notes, being aware that we had to take a decision, as we were due for a coffee break at four. The South Africans spoke again and gave me the impression that they were not going to vote against the motion. Most of their comments were related to the boycott and at not being able to participate. Then John Kendall-Carpenter made a strong dramatic intervention in favour of an RWC tournament and it was clear from that that he was going to vote for it. This was a make or break meeting and having thought I've got a majority here, I decided to call for a vote. "No point in going on," I said. "Gentlemen, we have been discussing it all day and I have 25 other points on the agenda. Now I am going to take a vote on the motion." John counted the votes and said, "Mr Chairman, the motion is passed." I said "We'll break for coffee now," and that was it.'

Two factors had convinced the Sydney hospital director to become such a formidable advocate of the RWC. First and foremost was the threat of what became known as the David Lord Professional Circus, an attempt by Australian journalist David Lord to launch a professional circuit. Second was the belief that rugby was engaged on an inexorable move towards professionalism and that it was important that the IRB remained in control of the game.

FACING PAGE David Kirk, who lifted the Webb Ellis Cup at the first RWC in 1987 as captain of the victorious All Blacks, holds the trophy once again in 2007 as it makes a tour of the four countries to have won it since the competition's inception.

According to Bob Stuart, Dr Vanderfield and Ross Turnbull, New Zealand, Australia and France voted in favour of the RWC proposal, with Scotland and Ireland solidly against it. The accounts regarding the Welsh and English vote vary. The Australians claim that the Welsh

ABOVE The IRB council that voted in favour of the Rugby World Cup. Inset is French representative André Bosc.

FACING PAGE The New Zealand All Blacks score against France in the 1987 final on their way to becoming inaugural World Cup winners.

vote was split, with Rowlands opting in favour and Treharne against. They also say that the two English representatives went different ways, with Kendall-Carpenter voting in favour, and Agar against. Keith Rowlands begged to differ. 'I voted for and so did Gwylim Treharne, who belonged to the liberal wing of the WRU. We had been instructed by the WRU Committee to vote in favour, so I really think that Wales voted for the RWC. Regarding the RFU, though, I am less sure about the way Albert Agar cast his vote. I somehow recall that both had voted for.'

The way the South Africans voted was also quite unclear, and the most credible account was that of Dr Vanderfield, who has been adamant that the South Africans simply did not vote. As Dr Fritz Eloff explained, South Africa tried to keep the door open, which would enable a way back into the fold should the boycott against South Africa be repealed or eased. However, at the end of the meeting, Bob Stuart confessed to being confused by the meaning of the vote. 'When we adjourned it was not quite clear what all this meant,' he said.

This was something Dr Vanderfield was well aware of. Such a vote could mean a lot if followed up by resolute movement, or very little if no action were taken. The IRB had committed itself 'by a majority to accept the principle of an International Tournament to be staged in 1987, as outlined …

but subject to it being under the control of the International Board. A condition was that the argument was for one tournament and that it was to be reviewed as soon as practicable after the event.' What was needed, reckoned Vanderfield, was the structure to move the project on. During the break he launched himself into a bout of frantic corridor diplomacy – in other words, into an attempt to put together an IRB Tournament Committee to take the matter forward.

'John Kendall-Carpenter was the ideal man to chair the Tournament Committee, which had to have an Australian and a New Zealander as members, as the organising unions. I also reasoned that we should have someone who voted against it, so I spoke to Ronnie Dawson, who had voted against. I knew him from the British Lions and I knew him to be dead honest about things. He said yes. Keith Rowlands was another one, as he had voted for,' Dr Vanderfield recalled.

'After coffee, I proposed the committee – Bob Stuart for New Zealand, Ross Turnbull for Australia, Dawson, Rowlands and Kendall-Carpenter – and they all said yes. The mechanics were sorted out, after which I said that there were various concerns of which I had a list. "Would you like to consider them now?" I asked. I anticipated the response and someone said they should be referred to the new committee. Agreed, [we] went on to next business.'

The choice of the people on the committee proved to be crucial – in particular that of John Kendall-Carpenter, a man of remarkable intellect and vision – as they made the difference between the success of the venture and the possible failure, observed Vanderfield. 'John Kendall-Carpenter was an outstanding leader who had a global dream, and although the Rugby Football Union did not want the World Cup, he did, and made it happen,' he added.

The tournament became a reality, and the men who voted for as well as against it have entered history; so have the dynamic duo of Sir Nicholas Shehadie, at the time president of the ARU, and New Zealander Dick Littlejohn, a leading NZRU council member. As passionate advocates of the RWC project, they became known as the 'Nick and Dick act' during their two-year lobbying spree around the world.

Avoid the ruck.

Private terminal.

30 minute check-in.

Only 100 passengers.

New York from £999 rtn flySILVERJET.com

INTERNATIONAL SCENE

Matt Giteau
More Than a Jack of All Trades
by RAECHELLE EDWARDS

'Giteau is a menace in attack, and opposition teams struggle to contain him when he's got ball in hand. He is also exceptionally versatile'

Matt Giteau is the highest-paid athlete in any Australian football code after signing with the Western Force in 2006. His three-year deal with Perth's Super 14 team is reportedly earning him the tidy sum of 4.5 million Australian dollars. Is he worth the money? Is he a genuine superstar of the game vital to the Australian revival, or is he a lone star without enough support?

There is no doubt that Giteau has a gift. 'I've always had a saying that you can't put in what God left out and Giteau was standing at the front of the queue when it comes to talent,' says Australian attack coach Scott Johnson. 'And to be able to do what he does – to play the 9, 10 and 12 positions – bears testament to the amount of talent he has. When you have players of that calibre, to really compete on the world stage, you want them fit, healthy and playing well.'

Giteau is a menace in attack, and opposition teams struggle to contain him when he's got ball in hand. He is also exceptionally versatile, and that is a huge advantage to any team he plays for, since it gives them plenty of options. At only 24 years of age, he is one of the mainstays of the Wallabies' back line. Rated among the world's best in his customary number 12 jersey, he has also shone for the Wallabies at fly half and successfully made the switch to scrum half for the 2006 spring tour. In the Wallabies' two Tests on home soil against Wales in May and June 2007, Giteau started at No. 9, but on both occasions the Aussie team, and particularly the back line, settled better when George Gregan entered the game from the bench at half back.

Giteau says he prefers playing inside centre. The Wallabies use him as a second five-eighth, in the Kiwi model. He is obviously comfortable playing alongside Gregan, Stephen Larkham and Stirling Mortlock. 'Being a part of the Brumbies for a number of years before moving to the Western Force ... I have a really good understanding of how they like to play.' And versatility can be a curse, 'if you're too versatile you become the perfect bench player'. Giteau says that his main goal is to secure one spot and not be so much of a utility player.

Giteau is becoming increasingly critical for the Wallabies in the lead-up to their World Cup campaign, with the many changes and experiments resulting in a back line that has struggled to find its rhythm. The Wallabies' coach, John Connolly, said, 'Giteau is a real thread of gold in the team; he is a world-class player, whether he plays 9 or 12, so he would be a massive loss [if injured].

'We have to keep our best players on the field and if we can we will be in the mix. If three or four of our backs, who are world class, Matt Giteau or Stephen Larkham or Stirling Mortlock or Lote Tuqiri, get injured we will be struggling to replace those.'

ABOVE Matt Giteau kicks a penalty for Western Force against the Sharks at Perth in the 2007 Super 14 competition. The Force won the match 22-12 against the eventual finalists, with Giteau clocking up five penalties and the conversion of Cameron Shepherd's try on his way to the man of the match award.

FACING PAGE Professional on the field but a bit mischievous off it. Giteau plays up to the camera during an autograph signing session at a Wallabies Fan Day at Manly Oval in May 2007.

ABOVE Giteau started at scrum half in the Tests on Australia's 2006 tour north. Here he is in action in the Wallabies' 44-15 win over Scotland at Murrayfield.

Giteau explains that he won't do anything differently in the lead-up to the World Cup, claiming that injuries happen when you try too hard to protect yourself. He will employ the same principles he always has to 'try to recover the best you can from a match and try to prepare the best you can'. But the Wallabies' coaching staff were quick to rest him for their 2007 Test match against Fiji in Perth to give his slight knee injury a chance to heal.

Giteau's goal in the World Cup is 'personally to play well, but being in the squad, my goal is the team goal of winning the World Cup. It's a similar situation to 2003 when the Australian side was written off very early, and it came down to a field goal towards the end – we were that close to winning it. We have definitely still got that drive and that belief within us that we can win it and I think we've certainly got the players.'

Western Force coach John Mitchell commented, 'Giteau has a disciplined approach to professionalism; he knows what his body responds to so he puts in the necessary work … he maximises his time efficiently and has the self-awareness to adjust his game.'

Mitchell feels that Giteau, a relatively small man by current player standards at just over 5ft 10ins (178cm) tall, is best left to take the game as it comes, since one quality that makes him so special is his natural vision and ability to read the play.

'If they want to get the best out of his development as he goes on they won't want to choke him through structure. If they understand that he has the self-awareness to adjust his game and if they let him play what's in front of him, you'll always have a super footballer.

'Another great asset he has is he sees himself as an equal team member; he sees the team as coming first, and he recognises all the little pieces that determine good outcomes.' Giteau's ability to remain selfless will be an important factor in the Wallabies' drive to succeed.

Giteau had a relatively rapid rise to fame. After representing the Australian Sevens and Under 21 teams in 2001, he was a surprise selection on the Wallabies' spring tour of 2002, having never played a Super 12 game, and made his Test debut as a replacement against England at Twickenham at 19 years of age. In 2003, he scored a hat-trick of tries in Australia's Test start against Namibia and came on as a replacement in the World Cup final. He also made his Super 12 debut for the Brumbies that year.

In 2004 Giteau established his place in the Wallaby starting XV and was named as one of the five best players in the world. He ran on in the number 12 jersey in 11 of the 12 matches, and was also a key member of the victorious Brumbies Super 12 team, a highlight of his career. The following season, his ten Test caps included two outings in the number 10 jersey, one of which was a man of the match performance in the

BELOW Giteau is congratulated by George Gregan and Clyde Rathbone after scoring for the Brumbies in their 47-38 victory over the Crusaders in the 2004 Super 12 final.

ABOVE Matt Giteau receives the Try of the Year award at the 2006 John Eales Medal evening in Sydney for his second try in the 49-0 defeat of South Africa at Brisbane that July.

RIGHT A cheeky Matt Giteau turns to smile at the defence as he dives in for a score against Wales in the first Test at Sydney 2007.

Wallabies' 74-7 victory over Samoa; he won a further man of the match award, this time from inside centre, in the following Test against Italy, which Australia won 69-21.

In 2006 Giteau played in the Australian Sevens team in the Commonwealth Games but missed the opening three Tests of the season with a knee injury. He announced his return to Test rugby with a two-try haul and a man of the match performance, once again from inside centre, in the Wallabies' record 49-0 win over the Springboks in Brisbane in the Tri-Nations. It was later that year, on the Wallaby spring tour – which formed part of the northern hemisphere autumn international series – that John Connolly experimented by switching Giteau to scrum half, starting him in all four Tests in the number 9 jersey. By that point he was on his way to Western Force, and in 2007, his first season there, Giteau scored 71 points in the Super 14 to take his Super 12/Super 14 career tally past 200. He also played his fiftieth match in the competition that season, against his former team, the Brumbies, in Canberra.

Giteau's sporting success has been matched by his sister Kristy, who has represented Australia in both rugby union and rugby league, while his father, Ron, captained the Canberra Raiders rugby league side. Off the field, Matt is not conventional. A mischievous lad, he regularly dyes his hair

different colours and enjoys shopping for the latest fashions. John Mitchell loves Giteau's cheekiness and passion. 'His enthusiasm is infectious among the group, and he brings a lot of energy and natural leadership through his actions.' And Scott Johnson explains, 'The beauty of Matt, he's got a great balance between the Australian rogue we love off the field but he's got the professionalism that his sport demands on the field.'

Winning the Webb Ellis Cup in 2007 is going to be a very tough assignment for the Australian side, and Giteau is crucial to their chances. They are only in with a shot at victory if he is fit and has top-level support around him, and if the Wallabies are blessed with plenty of luck along the way. As for the dollars and his worth, Scott Johnson sums it up: 'I don't care what you get paid, I care how you represent it, and I think Matt Giteau represents the money he earns in a really good way that his family would be proud of.'

Portugal's Miracle
Los Lobos Win Through to France

by **CHRIS THAU**

'It was refreshing, said an old rugby hand, after the cynicism of professional sport to listen to amateur sportsmen ... explaining their remarkable achievement in simple terms'

The arrival of Portugal among the elite of world rugby is regarded by both local pundits and outside observers as nothing short of a miracle. The Portuguese sporting landscape is dominated by soccer to such an extent that the success of the Portuguese rugby team in reaching the finals of the Rugby World Cup for the first time was treated with some incredulity, before it percolated through to the pages of the media, who belatedly gave it headline treatment.

Portugal reached the finals via the Repechage process, having failed to secure one of the three European qualifying slots on offer. In the final stages of the European qualifying rounds, Italy were first to qualify as Europe One, followed by Romania and eventually Georgia as Europe Two and Three respectively. Portugal, mauled by Italy, were sent back to the drawing board. But the Portuguese players were determined to avoid this time the narrow failures of 1998, when the Portuguese team, at the time coached by the flamboyant João Paulo Bessa, came tantalisingly close to reaching the 1999 finals, and of 2002, when Iberian arch-rivals Spain brought their dreams of travelling to Sydney the following year to a swift end.

In the first round of the Repechage against Morocco, the African runners-up, Portugal steeled

themselves to beat them twice, winning the away game 10-5 in Rabat as well as the home leg 16-15. The Uruguay job was even tougher as the Portuguese Lobos (Wolves) entered the final clash in Montevideo defending a slender seven-point margin, having won the first leg 12-5 in Lisbon. It was a battle of attrition in which the character and the defensive skills of the Portuguese, a bit of good luck as well as the haste and errors of the Teros played their part. Portugal managed to stay alive by one point, on aggregate, having lost the encounter 18-12. The advice of consultant coach Daniel Hourcade of Argentina proved essential in creating the platform to secure the much-desired result after a dramatic finale.

As the story of the success of the Portuguese rugby team broke, the emergence on the TV screens and in the pages of the media of the level-headed, modest young gentlemen of rugby was a breath of fresh air. It was refreshing, said an old rugby hand, after the cynicism of professional sport to listen to amateur sportsmen – students, accountants, engineers and doctors, playing sport for the love of the game – explaining their remarkable achievement in simple terms like passion, pride, dedication and commitment. In a short while the Portuguese rugby team became the darlings of the media, with features in almost all publications and TV reports and documentaries.

In Portugal, rugby is the 'in' sport, though for how long, no one knows. Some horrific defeat in the RWC may change all that, though the players will do everything in their power to prevent it. The Portuguese 'Wolves' are the genuine amateur team of RWC 2007, with the vast majority of the side's

> **LEFT** The final whistle goes in Montevideo and Portugal have qualified for the RWC 2007 finals tournament in France, having prevailed over Uruguay 24-23 on aggregate.

components working and playing their rugby in Portugal. A few exceptions exist, with the likes of Gonçalo Uva of Montpellier, André Silva of Nimes and David Penalva of Blagnac playing in France.

Reaching the RWC is an achievement that the architect of Portugal's ascent, coach Tomaz Morais, described as 'a step too far', painfully aware of the huge gap in standard and playing resources between his country and pool opponents New Zealand, Scotland, Italy and Romania. 'Make no mistake, we will prepare like never before for the tournament and the Federation is fully behind us. But it is a question of simple mathematics,' Morais added.

'We don't have the numbers, the structure and the finance to match the likes of New Zealand, Scotland and Italy. The gap between the domestic level and the international standard in the leading countries is not that great. Stade Français could give France a good game, so could Auckland if they play New Zealand. In Portugal, there is no domestic team capable of matching the National Team. The gaps are too big. That is reflected at international level. However, we are not concerned about scores in RWC, though a defeat by 50-60 points against the likes of New Zealand I would describe as a good result for us. We will do our best against Italy and Scotland, and regard the game against Romania as our legitimate target.'

ABOVE João Uva struggles to break free of Morocco's Mehadji Tidjani during Portugal's 16-15 victory in Lisbon.

LEFT Coach Tomaz Morais is realistic about what Portugal can hope to achieve in France.

The Giant Awakens
the Resurgence of South Africa
by RAECHELLE EDWARDS

'So what has changed? What has happened to the mindset and aptitude of South African players to move them from being considered the easy-beats in the Super 12 and Super 14?'

As Super 14 2007 came to a close, the warning bells started ringing in rugby nations around the world: it was the first ever all South African final. The Bulls and the Sharks battled it out in a nail-biter, with Springbok wing Bryan Habana scoring a try two minutes into injury time to lead the former to a thrilling win for their first Super 14 title. Bulls fly half Derick Hougaard added the conversion, to spoil the party for the Sharks' 54,000 home fans. The Bulls had triumphed 20-19, after trailing 14-10 at the break.

ABOVE Bryan Habana sails past fellow Springbok J.P. Pietersen to score the winning try as the Bulls beat the Sharks 20-19 in the final of Super 14 2007.

Everyone on the international stage had started to take serious notice in September 2006 of what was happening in South African rugby. In the final two Tri-Nations games, which took place that month, the Boks defeated the All Blacks 21-20 at Royal Bafokeng Sports Palace, Rustenburg, and

LEFT Sharks scrum half Ruan Pienaar leaves Phil Waugh of the Waratahs in his slipstream.

BELOW No-side at Rustenburg in the 2006 Tri-Nations, and the Springboks have defeated the All Blacks 21-20.

then beat Australia 24-16 at Ellis Park. The former result signalled that South Africa weren't fearful of New Zealand, which was an important mental shift.

A cracking Super 14 season has since followed in 2007, which put South Africa on a psychological high. A wave of optimism swept through the republic, and the Boks convincingly thrashed England at home in the two Tests in late May/early June – by 48 points (58-10) in the first; in the second they were victorious 55-22.

There is consensus at the top level of southern hemisphere rugby that it is a good thing that the Boks 'are back'. Both coaches and players have seen South African rugby's return to form as important for the game, and are almost relieved that the traditional strength of the once-mighty Springboks remains. 'Psychologically [winning the Super 14] is a massive boost for them; I think it's given them the opportunity to grow another leg, which is great for the game. I think it has been quite refreshing for the game to see them have success,' said Western Force Super 14 coach and former All Black John Mitchell. Meanwhile, Scott Johnson, Australia's attack coach, opined, 'I think everyone in rugby has had a great fear that if South Africa got their system right they'd be bloody hard to beat.'

So what has changed? What has happened to the mindset and aptitude of South African players to move them from being considered the easy-beats in the Super 12 and Super 14 to the big improvers over the past 18 months? Mitchell maintains that what we are now seeing is long-term planning coming to fruition. 'Things don't happen overnight ... they take time to grow ... if you look at Heyneke Meyer's plan, the Bulls were on the bottom of the Super 14 table for three seasons – they did not win a game in one season.

'He has had a player group together for five or six years and the success that they achieved tangibly has come from sustaining improvements and continuing the hunger.'

Mitchell also feels that the long coaching tenures have created stability. Jake White has been at the helm of the Springboks for more that 40 Tests.

Physically the players have improved. Conditioning has been top of the agenda for coaches looking for that edge over opponents. South Africa have traditionally had very big, powerful forwards. Now they are fitter, faster, smarter and they have enhanced skills. Their ability to offload the ball is making a difference.

'The influence of the Bulls' loose forwards and their No. 9 has been huge. They've got big 9s that are kind of like loose forwards and have exceptional kicking games,' Mitchell said.

'You look at the Bulls' loose-forward trio of Pierre Spies, Danie Rossouw and Wikus van Heerden … they're all big men that carry the ball. Likewise at the Sharks, you've got Ruan Pienaar and A.J. Venter and Ryan Kankowski. They are big men that can carry the ball and have a huge influence on attack and defence.'

Wallaby coach John Connolly agrees. 'They've got massive forwards, their back-line play is improving and they've got tremendous depth.

'They've had a number of internal issues settling down with the quota system and so forth … they have got a lot of depth, they have got a lot of young players coming through, and I think South African rugby is settling down as a general rule.'

This depth is critical as South Africa added a Super 14 team to their ranks and it has strengthened their system. They have got numbers, they've got athletes, they've got a genuine love of the game and players are being picked on form; no one has claims to any spot – that is a dangerous combination. Scott Johnson said, 'I was fortunate to be at the Under 19s carnival in Durban, South Africa, a few years ago and I saw the dawning of where the quota system was working.

'Through the last four or five years, with trying to get the coloured players into the game in South Africa you probably didn't have the quality, but three years ago when they won the Under 19s carnival the superstars of that very successful side were coloured … and it's not a limited game any more and because of that you're getting different athletic prowess in the coloured guys … some genuine speed, some great evasion skills … they're the ones who've come to the fore and what you're getting is a spreading of the talent base.'

The South Africans have also been more open to learning from others, to drive improvements, and they have not only improved defensively, but they can also boast a new-found ability to find space in attack. In October 2006, Bulls coach Heyneke Meyer head-hunted Australia's Todd Louden as attack coach to boost his side for the Super 14. The ex-Randwick coach brought a new element, getting the Bulls to do something new – to think for themselves.

'They weren't used to evolving and developing play. It was more authoritarian. They were very much told, "This is what you do and how you do it",' Louden said.

'Something I've been able to bring to the table is a different perspective. Now they go away and think about it and come back with various different views. They have really responded to having that input. And although we haven't forced tactics a hell of a lot this year, it has helped them be more flexible on the field.'

Rugby is truly the national sport in South Africa; they are fanatical and incredibly competitive, and the success of the Springboks impacts the national psyche. The South African team is in the same pool as England and Samoa in the Rugby World Cup and coach Jake White sees his side's emphatic victories over both nations in the lead-up as a 'psychological edge' on the way to the big tournament in France. 'Given that it is a Rugby World Cup year, it is paramount for us to maintain a winning momentum, and have the right mindset,' White said.

One of the stand-out images of Rugby World Cup history remains that of Springbok captain Francois Pienaar being handed the Webb Ellis Cup by Nelson Mandela, South Africa's first black president. More than recognition of sporting triumph, that victory in 1995 symbolised the beginning of the reconciliation of a nation that had been torn apart by apartheid. Banned from the first two tournaments by the international boycott, the Boks had made a dramatic return to the international scene. Only just beaten by Australia in the semi-finals of the 1999 Rugby World Cup and then defeated by New Zealand by 20 points in the quarter-finals of the 2003 World Cup in Australia, they began to rebuild. Now a genuine South African nationalism is emerging, and with it comes a united and real self-belief in the players and fans. This will propel the Boks as they ambitiously chase their second world title in four attempts. The giant that is South African rugby is now in full revival.

Strength in teamwork

Clifford Chance is pleased to support Wooden Spoon.

Our mission is grounded in the belief that we have a responsibility as a business
to contribute to our communities. For further details see our website:
www.cliffordchance.com/community

CLIFFORD
CHANCE

www.cliffordchance.com

Rising Stars
International Age-Grade Rugby 2007
by **ALAN LORIMER**

'Not unexpectedly, the final had been an all southern hemisphere affair, but thanks to Wales there was a European representative among the top four'

ABOVE South Africa's Wilton Pietersen bursts through a tackle to score his second try in his side's 32-18 semi-final victory over the Wallaby Under 19s.

FACING PAGE Rowan Kellam puts the brakes on Mathieu Bastareaud as Australia Under 19 beat France Under 19 30-11.

PAGE 47 Zach Guildford breaks clear to score against England Under 19. New Zealand Under 19 ran out 34-13 winners at Ravenhill, Belfast.

New Zealand returned to the top of Under 19 rugby after winning the IRB World Championship in Belfast last April with an emphatic victory over 2005 winners South Africa at Ravenhill in what was the last of these tournaments in this particular age-group. From 2008 there will be a rationalisation of the two IRB age-group competitions, with a single Under 20 championship replacing the global Under 19 and Under 21 competitions; Under 18 tournaments will be staged regionally. The thinking is that by the time players are in the Under 21 category they should already be in the professional set-up. Under 20 will now become the shop window for tomorrow's stars.

The Baby Blacks, runners-up for the previous two years, were determined to avoid a third consecutive second place, and in the event there was never much doubt they would finish on top of the pile. That certainty increased at the end of the pool stage, from which New Zealand emerged as the leading nation, with three wins from three games and bonus points in each.

Wales offered most resistance before losing 37-14, while England succumbed with a 34-13 scoreline. In between, the Baby Blacks showed no mercy to Japan, hitting the ton with a 107-6 slaughter.

New Zealand then had a rematch against Wales in the semi-finals, winning 36-12 to book a place in the final. Australia, the 2006 winners in Dubai, looked the likely side to join New Zealand after achieving a clean sweep in their pool games, but in the semi-finals the young Wallabies were brought to heel by a resurgent South Africa, whose 32-18 victory made them worthy finalists.

But any thoughts South Africa had of repeating their 2005 success in Durban were blown away in the opening minutes as New Zealand's whirlwind start reaped instant tries, leaving the Baby Boks in a hopeless position and eventually defeated 31-7.

It was a masterful display by New Zealand and depressing for the rest of the world, who could only watch another group of talented future All Blacks hog the stage at Ravenhill. Led by lock Chris Smith, who seems destined for higher honours, the New Zealand side was packed with potent players, the pick of them being full back Trent Renata (who bagged two tries and three conversions in the final), outside half Dan Kirkpatrick, wings Zach Guildford and Kade Poki, prop Ben Afeaki and No. 8 Liukanasi Manu. Watch out for these names in the near future.

Although well beaten in the final, South Africa still performed well throughout the championship. They too had a number of stars, among them full back Wilton Pietersen, centre Stefan Watermeyer and hooker Henri Bantjes.

Not unexpectedly, the final had been an all southern hemisphere affair, but thanks to Wales there was a European representative among the top four. Wales, who have performed well at Under 19 level in recent years, met defending champions Australia in the play-off for third and fourth places. At half-time Wales had every reason to think they were on course for a third-place finish. They led 21-10, only for the young Wallabies to stage a second-half fightback to finish winners 25-21, both sides scoring three tries.

For Wales, half backs Rhys Webb and Gareth Owen performed well and there were eye-catching displays from centre Tom Williams and No. 8 and captain Sam Warburton. Australia's side featured future stars Brett Gillespie at outside half, Sam Wykes at lock and Ben Daley at tight-head prop.

Earlier on finals day, expectations had been for an England win over France in the fifth/sixth play-off match. But in the event France, who had blown hot and cold in the earlier rounds, steadied their temperature to turn on a skilful display of running and offloading to outplay the men in white. France, winners 43-17, were well served by the powerful running of their bulky centre Mathieu Bastareaud, who scored two tries against England, as well as by skilful outside half Mathieu Belie, of whom more will be heard in the future.

For England, it was a disappointing end to a tournament in which matters had gone wrong in the pool stages, where the two wins – over Samoa and Argentina – had yielded no bonus points. Nevertheless, in defeat England can look to a number of players coming through the system, notably centre Alex Tait and scrum half Richard Bolt.

If England struggled to overcome Samoa in the pool stages, then that was no surprise. The Samoans have been helped by investment from the IRB, and that infusion of cash has certainly paid off in terms of a much more structured game that was enough to take the Pacific islanders to a 13-12 win over Argentina in the seventh/eighth play-off.

One level lower, it was hosts Ireland and their Celtic cousins Scotland who were battling it out for ninth and tenth places. The two countries had met in the pool stages, with Ireland grabbing a 13-12 victory with a last-gasp score and conversion. In the second meeting, however, Ireland produced their best performance of the tournament, dominating proceedings to win 34-0 with fine displays from centre Jamie Smith, outside half Scott Deasy and flanker Paul Ryan. For Scotland, who have struggled at Under 19 level in the past few years, prop Joe Stafford, flanker Fraser McKenzie, outside half Ruairidh Jackson and wing Lee Jones laid down markers.

In the remaining match, for eleventh and twelfth places, Fiji had little difficulty in racking up a large score against the Division A whipping boys, Japan, to win 60-12.

While the IRB Under 19 World Championship took centre stage, the Under 18 Six Nations tournament

RIGHT New Zealand Under 19 prop Ben Afeaki on the drive during the semi-final against Wales Under 19. The Baby Blacks won 36-12 to book a place in the final and eventually become world champions.

was being played out in Glasgow. This was not a championship but a festival, in which each of the six teams played only three games in the space of a week. All the same, it provided fierce competition and a chance for younger players to attract interest. In the event none of the big sides achieved three wins from their three games. England, Wales, Ireland and Scotland all finished with two wins; France and Italy had one each.

Wales had looked in form after defeating France 30-16 and then England 21-9 before losing their 100 per cent record in the final round. Yet Wales can look to utilising talented players in the future, notably outside half Dan Biggar and centre Jason Harries.

For hosts Scotland, there was a 15-6 defeat by England in their opening match, but thereafter the Scots found their form to defeat Italy 20-17 and then record a rare win over Wales, 20-13, on the final day of play. There are now signs that the Scottish academy system is producing future stars, the pick of them being scrum half Andy Dymock, full back Steve Aitken and flanker Chris Fusaro. For England, meanwhile, wing Sebastian Stegmann and outside half Rob Miller put their hands up for future notice.

The Best By Far
the Hong Kong Sevens 2007

by IAN ROBERTSON

'It is about the "haves" and the "have nots" of world rugby. The big fish and the minnows share the same pond for one wonderful weekend'

When I covered the Cathay Pacific Hong Kong Sevens for the BBC for the first time in 1981, I recognised then it was the best Sevens tournament in the world by some considerable distance. Nothing has changed in the intervening 26 years. Cathay Pacific remain the sponsors, and it is still far and away the best Sevens tournament.

In a curious way it is a bit like the RBS Six Nations Championship. The rugby is very important, but it is about more than just the rugby. A Six Nations weekend in Dublin or Paris or Rome or

anywhere is about the whole occasion. It is about the banter and the 'crack' from the Friday morning to the Sunday night.

It is one glorious party over three very special days. And the Hong Kong Sevens is exactly the same. In fact in Hong Kong, for those with a strong constitution the festivities last a week. The increasingly popular and highly successful 'Tens' tournament has created its own special niche on the Wednesday and Thursday. There are various lunches and dinners throughout the week, and the Sevens at the weekend caps it off in style. The weekend is a magnificent kaleidoscope of colour, pageantry, noise and action (see pages 54-55). The 'South Stand' rocks to the beat of the music, highlighted by the Cathay Pacific and Credit Suisse adverts. The eccentric costumes of the Sevens party-goers make it all about fun.

The rugby, of course, is the centrepiece. It is about the 'haves' and the 'have nots' of world rugby. The big fish and the minnows share the same pond for one wonderful weekend. What's more, occasionally the minnows have their 15 minutes of fame. In 2007, little Tunisia surpassed themselves. They beat mighty France 21-12 and nearly beat Australia. Tonga rattled up 33 points in beating Wales, and two of the world's political superpowers but rugby dwarfs – Russia and China – notched up notable wins over Italy and Canada respectively. Indeed Russia went on to win the Bowl final, comfortably beating France 21-7. The flag for the Home Unions was carried by Wales. They beat Argentina 26-19 to win the Plate final.

As for the final of the Cup, there was a shock victory for Samoa over Fiji. The favourites for the Cup, Fiji and New Zealand, had met in a ferocious, brutal, energy-sapping semi-final. Fiji won 21-12, but they looked drained and exhausted at the end. On the other hand, Samoa cruised through their semi-final against South Africa 10-0, without needing to go into overdrive, and that left them fresh for the final, which they won 27-22. Samoa's win was proof if proof were needed that Sevens rugby is often unpredictable. Fiji's defeat cost them dear in the annual World Sevens Championship. With victory in Hong Kong, they would have finished top of the table. But Fiji's finishing runners-up in Hong Kong and losing dramatically 21-14 in the quarter-finals to Wales in the last event of the calendar at Murrayfield meant New Zealand were crowned champions by the narrowest of margins.

FACING PAGE Chae Jae-Young of South Korea gets away from Argentina's Santiago Gomez Cora on day one in Hong Kong.

ABOVE Two months later in a stadium far, far away, the All Blacks celebrate becoming IRB Sevens champions after their 34-5 victory over Samoa in the final of the Murrayfield event.

New experiences keep us young and maintain our sense of wonder. Only by travelling can we explo

live in. Move farther with Cathay Pacific to over 120 destinations worldwide. You never know wl

call 020 8834 8888 or visit www.cathaypacific.co.uk

Move farther

…he many cultures and people that make up the world we …

…you'll see until you're there. To fly Cathay Pacific,

CATHAY PACIFIC

Now you're really flying

Rugby on the Move
England Under Brian Ashton

by **MICK CLEARY**

'Ashton is more than a man with a clever mind. Don't, if you value your life, ever accuse him of being an airy-fairy, expansive coach … a sort of pinko on the rugby pitch'

There are certain things you should avoid doing with Brian Ashton. One, don't use the term 'ball carrier', the trot-out cliché that most have employed from time to time: 'He's a great ball carrier, that one.' 'So what?' Ashton will retort. 'Anyone can carry a ball.' Fair enough, Brian. Decent point.

Ashton's not too keen on tackle bags, either. Line up four tackle bags and ask a bunch of kids what they see in front of them. Most will reply 'Four tackle bags'. The one that says 'Space either side of the tackle bags' is the one who will make Ashton's squad.

Ashton is more than a man with a clever mind. Don't, if you value your life, ever accuse him of being an airy-fairy, expansive coach, one who believes in free expression and creativity and liberalism, a sort of pinko on the rugby pitch. Ashton is a rugby coach. Full stop. If the best way to get the better of the opposition is to beat the living daylights out of them up front, then that is what should be done. If the strength of the side is up front, and the back line is struggling, perhaps with injury or a distinct lack of familiarity, or you're facing a team with seven Jonah Lomus across the back line and a gang of pansies in the pack, then keep it tight.

Ashton's way is the intelligent way: it's rugby on the move, it's rugby that demands a sense of responsibility from each and every player on the field and engages them all in that process of interaction and assessment. 'What's the game plan, Brian?' is one of those inquiries that gets swatted back over the net pdq. 'Game plan? I don't know. I'm not playing.'

The players are given a framework of various reference points. They then have to work it out for themselves. Quite right, too. What's the point of a rigid game plan if you don't know what the opposition are going to do at any given moment? You might think you know, from all those endless hours spent in front of a DVD player watching in-depth technical analysis of previous games, but you don't actually know.

One of my own pet hates is when coaches attempt to explain away their side's pitiful showing by moaning that the opposition slowed the ball down. Well, of course, they did. What do you expect them to do? Roll over meekly. Those chalk marks on the dressing-room blackboard have a horrible habit of turning into grizzly, 17-stone, uncooperative pains in the backside.

So much for the idiot's guide to the Ashton methodology. He's not a romantic. Far from it. He's an arch-realist, as has been shown by the firefighting job he's been doing with England ever since he took over from Andy Robinson at the turn of the year. Ashton has had little time to really mould a side to his own inclinations. He has had to make do and mend in order to get England out of the hole into which they had toppled so unceremoniously in autumn 2006.

Andy Robinson was a good forwards coach but was undermined both within and without by various circumstances. Injury is the bane of any coach's tenure. Robinson was unlucky on that front. Ashton's first game in charge, against Scotland in February, saw Jonny Wilkinson, Mike Tindall and Andy Farrell in action.

Robinson was also hampered by the daft, cobbled-together itinerary, one that saw an extra game scheduled, against New Zealand of all things, to mark the opening of Twickenham's South Stand. Six days later came Argentina, a game the beleaguered Robinson could not afford to lose. What happened? Yes. England lost.

Political matters appear now to be far less intrusive and disruptive. England had reached rock bottom – or so they hoped after defeat to South Africa, their eighth loss in nine games – and realised that something drastic had to be done. Ashton set about rectifying technical coaching issues while Rob Andrew was charged with sorting out the political turf wars that had so scarred the landscape of English rugby.

Ashton's appointment, on a long-term contract rather than as some stop-gap solution until the World Cup was over, or until some fancy-dan overseas coach could be secured, surprised some people. Those who knew him well were not surprised. Ashton has always been a rugby man's man. He doesn't do spin or side issues or mind games. He's a coach.

Former England Grand Slam-winning coach Dick Best was a fan. 'I hope that the RFU now don't even contemplate looking further,' said Best shortly after the news broke. 'Brian deserves a crack at being head

FACING PAGE England head coach Brian Ashton paces pensively during an England training session before the summer's second Test v South Africa at Pretoria.

coach. He's been coaching most of his life. Let's give the guy his head. No one has looked at him in all seriousness but thought of him more in a holding role until something better might come along. Why? Brian ticks all the boxes. Let's see what he's made of.'

Ashton already had experience in the Test arena as head coach. He took up the Ireland job in 1997 after seven years with Bath in tandem with Jack Rowell. Ashton's time with Ireland was not a happy one as he fought constant battles with those who objected to seeing an Englishman in the role. His relationship with manager Pat Whelan was always a tricky one.

Within a year, Ashton had resigned. He was then brought on board by Clive Woodward and helped nurture England's attacking play through to 2002. After that he worked with the RFU Academy and briefly with Bath again before being drafted in by the RFU following the clear-out of coaches last spring.

Ashton has handled the changeover in his customary unfussy, unpretentious way. He has not done anything radical or fancy. He has set the tone, stripping away some of the cumbersome support structures that surrounded the team and which he felt had induced something of a paralysis in the players' ability to think for themselves. A symbolic break with the recent past was also needed, and Ashton relocated the squad's training base to Bath. A new captain in Phil Vickery also represented a desire to start afresh.

Any coach, though, is defined by his selections, and throughout the Six Nations Championship, Ashton was bold. He backed young or inexperienced players such as Gloucester full back Olly Morgan and Harlequins back-row forward Nick Easter (it would have been Dan Ward-Smith but for a cruel cruciate injury befalling the Bristol No. 8 just prior to the start of the tournament) and expected them to repay his faith in them with some vibrant displays. We'll be seeing a lot more of these guys, as well as the Toby Floods and Shane Geraghtys, for a few years to come.

The regard in which Ashton was held can be gauged by the fact that Jason Robinson came out of international retirement to play Test rugby again. Lucky Ashton? No. Players want to play for him.

As England approach the World Cup, how has he laid down his markers? England's Six Nations Championship was middling. Victory over France was offset by a hammering at Croke Park by Ireland. Defeat on the final day by Wales, 27-18, suggested England had much to do.

The tour to South Africa saw two record defeats – 58-10 in Bloemfontein and 55-22 in Pretoria. No surprise there. England sent a fourth-choice pack of forwards and a mix 'n' match back line. In fact, the reality of both Tests was nothing like as one-sided and dispiriting as the scorelines might suggest. England, ravaged also by a mysterious stomach virus, gave heart and soul to the cause, even leading at half-time in the second Test in Pretoria. But they lacked the class and so the concentration to see it all the way through to the final whistle.

The South Africa trip was a tour to be endured. That there are 17 players from that trip in the extended England World Cup training squad is neither here nor there. The vast majority of those guys would have made the cut anyway. Those that did push themselves forward were hooker Mark Regan and prop Kevin Yates. Scrum half Andy Gomarsall did his cause no harm, either, which is more than can be said of Iain Balshaw and James Simpson-Daniel. Question marks as to their durability surfaced again on that tour and counted against them when it came to the training squad.

Ashton made one notable point as he wrapped up that arduous South Africa tour, namely that England lacked physicality. Cue the recall of Lawrence Dallaglio, the ageing warrior. His selection above all others ought to blow apart the myth of Ashton as some frothy practitioner. He's a pragmatist. He knows what it takes to win rugby matches. And if Dallaglio and Ronnie Regan and

Simon Shaw can gain the hard yards upon which the likes of Toby Flood and Mathew Tait might flourish, then so be it.

There were signs on that two-week trip to South Africa of England being well coached. There was a shape as well as a sense of purpose about them. Ashton has good coaching lieutenants in John Wells and Mike Ford.

England go to the World Cup in decent shape. And that is as good as it gets. They do not have a world-beating line-up to call on as Clive Woodward did four years ago. Check out the personnel. England had at least half a dozen certainties for a World XV in 2003. And today? None.

Ashton knows that. And he's prepared to go with that. A final point. The draw is in England's favour. Quarter-final against Wales or Australia. Into the semi-final. France, perhaps. Beat them in March. Into the final … Stranger things have happened.

Meeting Mathew Tait

by REBECCA BUTLER

'There is a certain air of his club and country team-mate Jonny about him when he begins to describe his fascination with only the negative points of his game'

We exit the top end of the N1, the deadly freeway that runs for 30 miles between Johannesburg and Pretoria, and head for Centurion. We are heading for the hilltop hotel where the England rugby team is staying in the run-up to the second Test match of the summer against South Africa. I say hotel, but with several of the guests battered by virus and injury the place resembles a sanatorium, full of infirm tourists. To add insult to injury, as it were, we are on our way to see a member of a touring side that was beaten – no stuffed – by a relentless Springbok outfit the week before. The nearer we get to the hotel, the lower our hopes become of a cheery encounter.

However, when we arrive the atmosphere is relaxed, and our man, the England centre Mathew Tait, is on fine form. And he has every reason to be. Despite the horrendous defeat England suffered the week before, Tait was the star of the match, displaying excellent ability and speed and making some breathtaking breaks.

Tait has obviously come a long way from that fateful day of 5 February 2005, when he was dump-tackled by Gavin Henson and taken off in England's opening Six Nations Championship game against Wales. When asked about his first cap, which made him, at 18 years old, the second-youngest player to appear for England since World War II, his memory is limited. He recalls lining up for the anthems and his parents' car window being put out in Cardiff but explains that the enormity of the situation, which thrust him into the media spotlight, did not dawn on him until much later. He is, however, hugely gracious about the incident, admitting that Henson's tackles were not 'car-crash tackles' and explaining that the decision to take him off was not personal but what Andy Robinson thought best for the team at the time.

Over the next two years, until he returned to the international arena, Tait enjoyed huge success with England on the Sevens circuit. His instinctive style of play and speed dominated the spacious environment of the game. This was a very important time for him, since he was able to rebuild his confidence and rediscover his love of rugby. Tait's return to the national side last season saw him play in the autumn internationals and be

---

LEFT Mathew Tait leaves the South African defence for dead during the first Test at Vodacom Park, Bloemfontein, at the end of May 2007.

involved in England's 2007 Six Nations campaign. His comeback has culminated in the personally very successful summer tour to South Africa.

Despite Tait's incredible performance on the tour, the ever-modest player confesses to becoming very frustrated with himself at times, for he believes that 'there is still more to come'. There is a certain air of his club and country team-mate Jonny about him when he begins to describe his fascination with only the negative points of his game and the need to work on every aspect of his rugby. His next goal in terms of rugby is establishing himself at 13 for England. How will he beat the fierce competition and achieve this? Simple answer. Get his head down and work hard.

Hard work does not stop at rugby in the life of Mathew Tait. In detailing a week of his routine at Newcastle, he casually mentions that he is currently doing a full-time degree in Biomedical Science at Newcastle University. He trains before and after lectures, attends daily team meetings at the club and studies in the evenings. He previously did two years of straight rugby but felt his brain was 'dying on him'. After achieving three grade As in Biology, Geography and Sports Science from Barnard Castle School, he thought he would give uni a go, with the academic aim of going into forensics.

A clearly hugely talented individual, Mathew Tait has a lot going for him. But off the pitch and out of the classroom, he also has an undeniable twinkle in his eye and a huge smile, and a very bright future ahead.

BELOW Wynand Olivier cannot escape Tait's clutches in the second Test at Loftus Versfeld, Pretoria, in early June 2007.

Summer Tours 2007
Wales in Australia

by GRAHAM CLUTTON

'The Wales squad came in for severe criticism from the Australian press as they arrived unnoticed with a bunch of what the locals described as "also-rans"'

Considering the aim, Wales arrived back from Australia in June with a collective smile. Admittedly, both Test matches against the Wallabies, in Sydney and Brisbane, ended in defeat, but for coach Gareth Jenkins, spending three weeks Down Under with the majority of his fringe internationals answered plenty of questions.

Having left 17 players behind for rest and rehabilitation purposes, the Wales squad came in for severe criticism from the Australian press as they arrived unnoticed with a bunch of what the locals described as 'also-rans'. Batting away the ill-advised comments, Jenkins took his side to within a few seconds of victory in the opening game

ABOVE Veteran Newport Gwent Dragons flanker Colin Charvis was outstanding for Wales in both Tests.

at the Telstra Stadium, and then despite losing 31-0 in the second, refused to lay the blame at the door of those who were clearly struggling from fatigue after a hectic end to the domestic season.

'I'm not sure why anyone was surprised with the make-up of the squad because we made it quite clear what our intentions were. Having said that, I was happy with the group of players we took and delighted when we were leading going into the last play in Sydney.

'Unfortunately, we couldn't go on and win it and then, in Brisbane, we ran out of steam. All in all, it was an excellent exercise and we were pleased with what we achieved.'

The absence of the likes of Dwayne Peel, Stephen Jones, Alun-Wyn Jones, Kevin Morgan, Tom Shanklin and Gethin Jenkins provided opportunities for others to stake their claim for a place in the World Cup squad. Youngsters Jamie Corsi and Tom James were also taken, for experience, whilst in the end injuries meant Worcester Warriors prop Chris Horsman was flown out a day before the second Test and played the final 30 minutes of the game.

Sadly, the game at the Suncorp Stadium will be remembered for all the wrong reasons, with the Cardiff Blues wing Chris Czekaj suffering a severe spiral fracture to his right leg. The 21-year-old was left behind to undergo surgery when the party flew back to Britain the following day. He eventually arrived back in Wales three weeks later to face a two-year rehabilitation programme. 'Our thoughts were with Chris and his family as we checked on to our flight and we wish him every success in his long recovery. He is a fine young player who will, without doubt, bounce back at the highest level,' said coach Jenkins.

Czekaj was one of the real success stories in Sydney as Wales rattled up a 17-0 lead inside as many minutes, courtesy of tries from captain Gareth Thomas and an interception from Blues centre Jamie Robinson. 'It was a great start and one which suddenly caught them cold,' said Thomas. Unfortunately, and despite James Hook's second-half penalty and dropped goal, Wales failed to hang on as replacement Stephen Hoiles crossed deep into injury time for Stirling Mortlock to convert.

Wycliff Palu and Nathan Sharpe scored the Wallabies' first two tries, but the host nation had been given a wake-up call by a bunch of so-called no-hopers. The pick, arguably, was Newport Gwent Dragons veteran Colin Charvis, whose outstanding performance on the blind-side flank all but sealed his place in Jenkins' World Cup party.

Gavin Thomas, the Scarlets open-side, who rarely gets the plaudits he deserves, was another individual who threw his hat into the ring, whilst Iestyn Thomas, the Scarlets loose-head, more than held his own in the scrum. That triumvirate and Dragons utility forward Michael Owen were the players who shone above anyone else. Owen, who had fallen from favour over the previous 18 months, was back to his best, carrying the ball with great purpose and showing quality in open play.

Injuries to Sonny Parker and Jamie Robinson meant both players were strapped up for the second Test in Brisbane seven days later, and although the former managed to

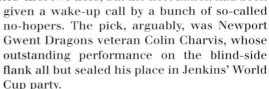

LEFT Jamie Robinson runs away to score for Wales in the first Test at Sydney.

FACING PAGE Wales were so close in Sydney, Stephen Hoiles crossing deep into injury time for the winning try.

survive a second physical pounding, Robinson was one of four first-half injuries that meant a serious reshuffle behind. In fact by the time half-time arrived, scrum half Michael Phillips was the only player still operating in his starting role. Gareth Thomas moved to the wing, Aled Brew switched wings, Hook switched from 10 to 12 and Parker moved from inside to outside centre.

'It was very unsettling, but not the reason why we lost,' said Jenkins. 'We stayed with them for 40 minutes, but when they brought on fresh legs in the second half, we were out for the count. They took their chances well, but I couldn't fault any one of them for their efforts.'

Charvis and Thomas were once again the pick of a decent bunch, despite the inability of the pack to provide a platform from first phase. The inclusion of Mefin Davies, a late replacement for Matthew Rees, who returned home to attend the birth of his first child, was supposed to improve the line out, whilst the addition of Horsman should have enabled Wales to build on their first Test domination at the scrum.

It wasn't to be. The line out was a shambles and the scrum was negated due to referee Paul Honiss' interpretation of the 'crouch, touch, pause and hold'. From driving back the Wallaby eight in Sydney, Wales found themselves consistently penalised for pausing too long before engagement. When they tried to reason with Honiss, their words appeared to fall on deaf ears.

As a result, Wales struggled for possession and found life increasingly difficult when replacement scrum half George Gregan came on at half-time and, in his own inimitable way, dictated from the base of a dominant pack. To their credit, Wales refused to drop their guard and continued to play with the tiny percentage of ball they could win at the set piece. Captain Thomas said, 'I told the boys at the end of the first Test that I was proud of their effort. I told them the same at the end of the second because they put in as much effort in Brisbane as they did in Sydney.

'It was just down to tiredness, we simply couldn't live with them in those final 30 minutes.

'However, anyone criticising this party should think again. I said all along that we should be judged on how we fare in the World Cup.'

Ireland in Argentina

by SEAN DIFFLEY

'The great irony was that Leinster's player of the year, the gifted Felipe Contepomi, skilfully dropped the winning goal for Argentina in the first Test'

Like the rest who ventured south during the summer, the Irish, with most of their senior players rested, were defeated, losing both Tests against Argentina. Of course the Pumas were not at full strength either but were more eager to make a point or two, since they face Ireland in their first pool game at the World Cup. Ireland coach Eddie O'Sullivan had seven uncapped

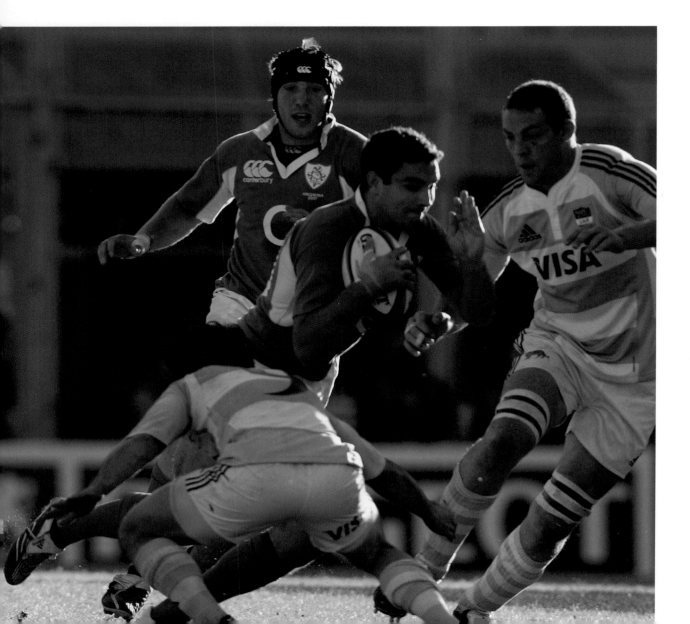

players in his squad, which was captained by prop Simon Best. 'Argentina is always a tough [place] to tour, but it gives us an opportunity to look at options with the World Cup in mind,' he said.

The experienced players in the squad included Geordan Murphy, Malcolm O'Kelly, who did not play in the Six Nations because of injury, Keith Gleeson, Mick O'Driscoll and wing Brian Carney, the recent recruit from rugby league. Out-half Paddy Wallace was injured in the first Test at Santa Fe, and there was a hurried call to the Churchill Cup side for Jeremy Staunton to fly out as the replacement for the second Test in Buenos Aires.

Not that it made a whit of difference. Brian Carney managed a score in the first Test, and that was the only try scored by the Irish. Overall, the two matches were pretty grim, mostly confined to heaving forward mauls and not of a very high standard. But Argentina managed without too much difficulty to keep the Irish back line ineffective. The great irony was that Leinster's player of the year, the gifted Felipe Contepomi, skilfully dropped the winning goal for Argentina in the first Test. Then, hastily changing in the dressing room, he managed to fly back to Dublin in time to receive his medical degree, the academic result of a few years as a student at Dublin's Royal College of Surgeons. Next season he'll be dropping goals again for Leinster.

As for Eddie O'Sullivan's World Cup options, the clear lesson from the Argentina tour was that Ireland, with its limited rugby populace, is not well off for candidates to bolster the number one players. The lack of skill displayed in Argentina was vastly disappointing, and one shudders to think of the immense gaps there would be if such as Brian O'Driscoll, Gordon D'Arcy, Paul O'Connell, John Hayes and their colleagues were to be injured before the events in France. Ireland's first choice stands high in the rankings, but signs for the future are not all that promising, even if the under age, the Under 19s and Under 20s, have revealed a good degree of talent. However, all that is very much in the future. Argentina was not a happy augury.

ABOVE Ireland try scorer Brian Carney is held this time by Esteban Lozada in the first Test at Santa Fe.

BELOW Simon Best and Malcolm O'Kelly (5) unite to halt Tomás De Vedia during the first Test.

FACING PAGE Ireland's Jeremy Staunton tries to go between Nicolas Vergallo and Rimas Alvarez in the second Test.

Churchill Cup

by HUGH GODWIN

That left a mere 55-metre run-in for … Tom Croft. It was no problem for the leggy 21-year-old, who left four covering Maori – Waldrom and three backs – in his mighty slipstream'

Had anyone been of a mind to borrow a slogan from football, the theme of the fifth Churchill Cup, sponsored for the second year by Barclays, might have been 'rugby's coming home'. With a World Cup in France to follow in the autumn, it was reckoned that the best location for the 2007 event was England not North America. So on the way to finals day at Twickenham, the good folk of Exeter, Stockport, Henley and Northampton played host to the A teams from England, Scotland and Ireland, plus the USA, Canada and Cup holders New Zealand Maori.

The tournament's two-week slot at the end of the domestic season coincided with that congested period of European club finals and international tours, when only the most attentive of us was quite sure who was coming or going, if at all. The upshot turned out to be of significant benefit to the Saxons, who were able to call on several top players from Wasps, Leicester and Bath who might in other years have been away with England. The three clubs' contingent – with the exception of Leicester's No. 8 Jordan Crane – were unavailable for the opening win over the USA in Pool A at Stockport. They entered the fray for the crucial pool match against Scotland A and were prominent in the Cup final triumph over New Zealand Maori at Twickenham.

To begin at the beginning, however, a crowd of around 6000 watched the Saxons – captained by the 37-year-old London Irish prop Neal Hatley, in his last matches before retiring – kick off the Churchill Cup with a 51-3 thrashing of the US Eagles. The Rugby Football Union – patrons of the event with their North American 'buddy' unions – were able to pitch Twickenham prices as they liked, but not at the club grounds, and Sale Sharks set their cheapest adult tickets at an arguably steep £22. The Eagles had most of their half-dozen European-based professionals available, but the Saxons scored almost at will and finished them off with tries in the last five minutes by the Newcastle pair of Phil Dowson at blind-side flanker and scrum half Lee Dickson.

RIGHT Salesi Sika of the USA is tackled by Canada full back Mike Pyke but seems aware that more trouble is about to arrive in the Bowl final at Twickenham on 2 June. Canada won the match 52-10.

There was a sense of the tournament building momentum – an identity, if you like – at Henley's Dryleas ground on a balmy Wednesday evening when the USA put on a much better show against Scotland A. The Scots began with ten full caps, which prompted Nigel Melville, the former England scrum half and captain who is now chief executive of USA Rugby, to suggest they were too strong. Frank Hadden, the Scotland coach, in charge of the A team as the senior squad were not touring, pointed out that he had 26 players resting or injured.

It seemed the USA might suffer fresh agonies when Scotland A's full back, Rory Lamont, ran in an early try. Fly half Gordon Ross converted and added a penalty for a 10-0 lead, but USA full back Francois Viljoen kicked three penalties for 10-9. The USA did well at the ruck while the Scots stole a few line outs. With some relief the Scots settled the result at 13-9 with another penalty by Ross, but he had broken a hand and was out of the tournament.

Pool B had kicked off with equally predictable outcomes but feistier rugby. Ireland A were typically uncompromising at the breakdown to quell a battling Canada, 39-20, at Exeter's superbly appointed Sandy Park ground. Canada's efforts earned them two tries, and they got another three when they met the Maori in front of another crowd of just over 6000 at Northampton. The New Zealanders, who had warmed up with a 'haka' at historic Rugby School, won 59-23 with nine tries, the first of them by flanker Scott Waldrom after fly half Callum Bruce charged down Canada full back Mike Pyke. There were seven conversions by Bruce, who thereafter ceded the number 10 jersey to Tamati Ellison with unfortunate consequences.

The Maori's second pool win, 50-22 over Ireland A at Exeter, could be summed up in the 58th-minute try scored by their galloping tight-head prop, Ben May. The Irish fumbled a behind-the-back pass and scrum half Chris Smylie showed them how it was done to instigate a direct and rapid counterattack that swept up the left touch line. The

BELOW Saxons hooker David Paice forces his way over for a try against Scotland A.

FACING PAGE, TOP The Ireland A Plate-winning side. The Irish prevailed over Scotland despite a last-ditch score from Thom Evans (*FACING PAGE, BOTTOM*).

Maori, Cup winners on each of their previous entries in 2004 and 2006, were through to another final to meet the England Saxons, who held off a Scotland side unable to deploy their planned wide game on a cold and rainy bank holiday afternoon at Twickenham.

The Saxons' head coach, Jim Mallinder, was a confident man before the Scotland match. 'We like to think we've got a pack to play in all conditions,' he said. So it proved as a try by London Irish hooker David Paice and a conversion and penalty by Bath's Olly Barkley gave the Saxons a 10-0 half-

time lead. Paice's try was set up by a sharp break from Nick Abendanon, the 20-year-old Bath full back soon to be summoned by England to South Africa. Abendanon scored himself after 43 minutes, hacking on Danny Cipriani's clever grubber. A penalty apiece by Calum MacRae and Nils Mordt left the Saxons winners 18-3.

Twickenham the following Saturday was, by contrast, dry and warm as all six teams mustered to contest, successively, the Bowl, Plate and Cup, competed for by the third-placed teams in each pool, the pool runners-up and group winners respectively. Canada, as in 2006, beat the USA for the Bowl, very comfortably 52-10, despite an opening try by the Eagles' Leeds prop Mike MacDonald. Scrum half Morgan Williams and No. 8 Sean-Michael Stephen shared four of Canada's eight tries, and the Canadians looked in much better shape for the World Cup than their neighbours.

Ireland A took the Plate with an attritional 22-21 defeat of the Scots. Frank Murphy, the Irish scrum half, back at the stadium where he had starred for Leicester in the Guinness Premiership final, charged down his opposite number, Rob Chrystie, for a try to help build a 12-3 advantage. But it was nip and tuck throughout, and when Scotland A's Glasgow wing Thom Evans – another with Twickenham memories from his Sevens exploits with Wasps – broke three tackles for a try in added time, there was the chance of a winning conversion. MacRae's effort drifted across the posts, though, and Ireland's captain, John Fogarty, collected the silverware.

Happily the main event was of high quality and no little incident. The Maori showed their customary and hugely laudable ability to run straight lines of support at pace. It is as if they operate to an unseen sheet of graph paper on the pitch, and the hard work they put in to make it happen would be well copied by others. The Maori had their faults, nonetheless, notably Ellison's inaccurate goal-kicking, and they were undermined further by the Saxons' clever defence, with Wasps' England wing Paul Sackey squeezing up and in at every opportunity.

Ellison missed three penalties and the conversion of wing Anthony Tahana's try, whereas Barkley converted Sackey's score from a classic counterattack off a lost Maori line out. Leading 7-5 at the interval, the Saxons sensed this could be their day. Ellison finally hit the target with a penalty, but a first-phase try off a scrum for Tom Voyce, with Cipriani gliding into the line from full back to take Mordt's long pass, made it 12-8 to the Saxons. The Maori went back in front with a 58th-minute try by centre Jason Kawau. The Saxons stuck to their guns, though, and won through with a try which might have come from the Maori playbook. An attack by the men in black broke down in the Saxons'

22, Voyce and Sackey shunted the ball as far as the 10-metre line, then Barkley flung a glorious cut-out pass to the right wing. That left a mere 55-metre run-in for the Leicester replacement lock, Tom Croft. It was no problem for the leggy 21-year-old, who left four covering Maori – Waldrom and three backs – in his mighty slipstream to bring the final score to 17-13 to the Saxons.

It was a try deserving a larger audience than Twickenham's 8324 spectators, and the Churchill Cup, which will return to North America in 2008 in Connecticut and Ontario, has work yet to do on that 'identity'. But Hatley's smile was a broad one as he lifted the Cup; and though it was an odd year in more than one sense, England were on top again in this tournament at least, after their successes in 2003 and 2005.

> *FACING PAGE* Tom Croft is congratulated by Matt Thompson after charging home from 55 metres.
>
> *BELOW* Saxon skipper and prop Neal Hatley savours Churchill Cup success before heading off into retirement.

Forward thinking

Investec is proud to support the Wooden Spoon. As a sponsor of England Rugby, Investec is looking ahead. We take an entrepreneurial approach to finance to achieve distinctive results. Providing a world-class range of private banking, asset management, investment banking and capital markets. For more information, please call **020 7597 4000** or visit our website **www.investec.com**

Australia • Botswana • Canada • Hong Kong • Ireland
Mauritius • Namibia • South Africa • Switzerland • Taiwan
United Kingdom & Channel Islands • United States

Private Banking
Asset Management
Investment Banking
Capital Markets

Out of the Ordinary™

HOME FRONT

By Their Fingertips
Worcester Stay in the Premiership
by CHRIS HEWETT

'As it was, it went to the wire – and a nasty stretch of barbed wire at that. Sixways was packed to the rafters for the big game with Saracens'

Twice in three years is twice too often, even if the fraught circumstances add an extra dimension to the Sixways experience. After eight long, frequently depressing months of Guinness Premiership rugby, Worcester reached the last day of the regular season trapped in a sporting cul-de-sac, with only one possible exit route. They could not be entirely sure that victory over a Saracens side with strong motivations of their own would keep them in the elite division, but they knew damned well that defeat would send them down. And if the players understood the nature of the challenge, having been in the self-same position at precisely the same stage of the 2004-05 campaign, it did not soften the moment. When the union game boils itself down to a win-or-bust imperative with jobs at stake, life is always granite-hard.

How had it come to this? The previous season, Worcester had done rather well for themselves in terms of consolidation. Having escaped relegation with a final-day victory over Northampton in the spring of 2005, their form the following autumn was sufficiently handy to earn them security by Christmas. Cecil Duckworth, the club's

LEFT Worcester's Samoan centre Dale Rasmussen comes up with the ball after scoring the Warriors' third try in their 22-7 last-day defeat of Saracens. The win ensured Premiership rugby at Worcester in 2007-08.

FACING PAGE Saints' Paul Diggin tries in vain to halt Drew Hickey as he drives for the line in the Warriors' 10-9 win at Franklin's Gardens on New Year's Day.

energiser-in-chief as well as its principal investor, extended the capacity at Sixways in the belief that business was in onwards-and-upwards mode. There were few significant additions to the playing staff, but the shifting of selected home games from Saturday afternoon to Friday night looked promising. Few visiting teams enjoyed the trip to the West Midlands in daylight. Presumably, they would enjoy it even less in the dark.

Yet within weeks, Worcester were in free fall. Bristol, whom they welcomed on the opening day of the season, put 40 points on them – the fruits of a clever close-season approach by their coach, Richard Hill, who started work a month earlier than everyone else in the confident belief that this would give his ageing forwards an important advantage. Worcester then travelled to Newcastle and built a winning lead for themselves before doing everything in their power to squander it. Somehow, the Tynesiders won 20-19. Over the ensuing weeks, it went from bad to worse. Sale, Gloucester and Northampton all won at Sixways; there was little in the way of respite at the Recreation Ground, Welford Road or the Stoop. Indeed, it was not until late November that they registered a Premiership victory, by squeezing a three-pointer past Saracens at Vicarage Road.

Reasons? Drew Hickey, the Australian No. 8 who had helped Worcester out of National Division One and into the top league in the first place, understood exactly what had happened. 'People make the mistake of thinking that the trouble started this season,' he said before that climactic game with Saracens, 'but our results have been pretty poor from Christmas 2005 onwards. It's been a struggle for 16 months now, and it's stifled us in terms of the way we play. It's difficult to move your rugby on, to extend and expand yourselves as a team, when the pressure to break a losing streak is there week after week. Bristol are a classic example of a side who have evolved. They've made good signings, they've brought a couple of new things to their act, they've generated some momentum

and they've played their way to the top end of the table. Us? We've fallen away, badly. It's not a great thing to admit, but it's true.'

It was Hickey who scored the try that made the difference, that persuaded Worcester that while they might be in deep strife, all was not lost. On New Year's Day, the team travelled to Northampton, who were also struggling, if not raging, against the dying of the light. Fresh set-piece laws had just been introduced – all that 'crouch, touch, pause, engage' nonsense that called for front-rowers to fondle each other gently and swap telephone numbers before crashing into the scrum – and on the face of it, they did no favours to Worcester's heavyweight exponents of grunt-and-groanism. Northampton, armed with two technically proficient scrummagers in Tom Smith and Pat Barnard, caused their opponents all manner of trouble, yet Hickey's driving try in the left corner earned him and his brethren a one-point victory. Suddenly, anything was possible.

BELOW The recovery continues. Warriors celebrate their 18-12 victory over reigning champions Sale Sharks at Edgeley Park on 9 March.

FACING PAGE (From left to right) Cecil Duckworth, Pat Sanderson and John Brain celebrate survival before the axe fell the following Monday.

By then, though, there had been a casualty at Sixways. Anthony Eddy, who had coached Hickey at Sydney University, lost his coaching job after that initial rush of poor returns. John Brain, the director of rugby, offered to resign around the same time but was turned down flat by Duckworth. 'Sooner or later, someone is held responsible for bad results,' Hickey recalled. 'That someone was Anthony. It seems that in English sport, there is always something unstable about a coaching job. It was hard for him, hard for his family, but what could the rest of us do except get our heads down and set about putting things right? At that point, the team could have gone completely tits-up – lots of infighting, that sort of stuff. We didn't allow that to happen.'

Phil Larder, the former England defence coach and one of the architects of the 2003 World Cup triumph, was now on board, flying in from his retirement home in Spain to run regular sessions. Together with Brain, whose game-analysis skills were considered to be as highly developed as anyone's, he began to build up the performance levels. There was a 3-3 draw with Wasps (not a thriller, it must be admitted, but hugely encouraging) plus a bonus point secured against Leicester. Bath were beaten at Sixways, Sale were vanquished in faraway Stockport, Newcastle were seen off in another tourniquet-tight game between the two outpost clubs. But for Craig Gillies' red-mist moment at Bristol in April – the outstanding lock gave an opponent some old-fashioned 'shoe pie' at the death and cost his side an attacking position that might easily have been translated into victory – they might have saved themselves with a fortnight to spare.

As it was, it went to the wire – and a nasty stretch of barbed wire at that. Sixways was packed to the rafters for the big game with Saracens, for whom victory might have meant a home tie in the semi-finals. Worcester did not give them so much as a sniff. Hickey scored again – when it comes to the important moments, he pops up with uncommon regularity – and there were further tries for Dale Rasmussen, the Samoan on whom the defensive structure had been raised, and a second Pacific islander, hooker Aleki Lutui. Job done. Now for next season.

Except. On the Monday following the big match, just as the bruises were yellowing and the hangovers were easing, Duckworth broke the news. Brain had been sacked. 'John has a massive reputation as a forwards coach and is considered to be one of the best in the Premiership,' the

SCOTLAND'S FINEST FLY HALF.

chairman said. 'The players have all clearly benefited from working with him and he has helped drive the club forward during his tenure. I would particularly want to praise him for his tremendous efforts in guiding the club away from relegation danger. But unfortunately, the results this season have not matched the levels we had all hoped for, and having debated the problem extensively ... the decision has been made to take the club forward under new leadership.'

The new leadership would be centred on Mike Ruddock, the former Wales coach who had taken the Red Dragonhood to a Grand Slam in 2005 before walking away from the job, weighed down and laid low by a virulent outbreak of player power. It emerged that Duckworth and the one-time Swansea flanker had been chewing the fat for some time. The chairman confirmed that he had talked Brain out of resigning in mid-season but also admitted to there being 'a question mark in that direction' that prompted the search for a contingency plan.

'I have always admired what Mike did with Wales,' he explained, 'and I always wondered what happened to his position there once he won the Grand Slam. I investigated that, and found it was really a couple of people working against him. Unfortunately, the management board in Wales accepted their view, which I am sure was sad for Wales and obviously sad for Mike. There was nothing more to it than that, so we met up. Then there was the question of whether or not we should parachute someone in if we continued to lose. We built our relationship, and then it became an issue of whether we should do it anyway at the end of the season, whether we were in the Premiership or National League One. Mike had said he would like the opportunity if I felt it was the way I wanted the club to go. People say: "Why would we want to change?" But I think the die had been cast. We didn't want to paper over some of the things that had gone wrong in the last 18 months. We felt it was time for a change.'

This was hard on Brain. Desperately hard. The Kingsholm-reared man of Gloucester had been at the very heart of Worcester's rise to Premiership standing, and clearly felt he had more to give, if his après-Saracens chat was anything to go by. He had attracted an All Black centre, Sam Tuitupou, to Sixways and had plans to strengthen the squad further. Whether or not those plans would have resulted in major improvements, we shall never know. Ruddock is now the man with the plans, and the money to finance them. He is nobody's idea of a fool. But then, neither was his predecessor.

RIGHT The new man at the helm at Worcester – Mike Ruddock, who guided Wales to a Six Nations Grand Slam in 2004-05.

Sunny in his Mind
Howard Takes Tigers to the Limit
by STEVE BALE

'Howard was known as a clever, creative individual with an awareness of space and rugby's endless possibilities. This he brought to his coaching at Leicester'

Nothing less became Pat Howard's heartfelt relationship with Leicester Tigers than his leaving of it – the Heineken Cup beating by Wasps that put an end to Leicester's treble chance and went a painfully long way to obscuring the triumphs that had gone before. Howard the player had been central to Leicester's great years of hegemony around the turn of the century. Howard the coach was responsible for nothing less than returning them to that pedestal after their place had been taken by those self-same Wasps.

These are achievements that will go down in Tigers history and are the more remarkable as Howard was an outsider who came into a club where the continuity provided by an endless stream of insiders – the likes of Dean Richards – had been an overriding strength. Ultimately it turned into not exactly a weakness but at least a double-edged sword. Leicester had already tried one eminent Australian when Bob Dwyer was their coach in the mid-1990s, and when Dwyer was sent on his way and they reverted to Richards, their suspicions appeared to have been confirmed.

LEFT Pat Howard watches the Tigers warm up before their 2007 Heineken Cup semi-final v Llanelli Scarlets at the Walkers Stadium in Leicester.

FACING PAGE Howard, with Austin Healey and skipper Martin Johnson, lifts the Zurich Championship trophy in 2001, his final playing season for the Tigers. The next week, he would sign off with success in the Heineken Cup final, a triumph he almost repeated as coach.

Then Leicester went on their four-year march through the Premiership under Richards, culminating in a league and European double in consecutive seasons. Howard played in the first three of those seasons, the 2001 Heineken final being his Tigers farewell. He went home for one last, abortive crack at regaining a place with Australia.

As a player, Howard had been rugby's equivalent of an infant prodigy, capped for the Wallabies at 19 and winning 20 caps at centre or fly half by the time he was 24. But it was his misfortune to be around at the tail end of Michael Lynagh's great career, and after 1997 Howard's Test career was over. Hence the wanderlust. At Leicester they are simply grateful that the Australian selectors should so wantonly have discarded so rich a talent. Even now, at 33, Howard looks fit and strong enough still to be playing the game, as proven by an appearance in a charity game at Northampton last season.

Howard was known as a clever, creative individual with an awareness of space and rugby's endless possibilities. This he brought to his coaching at Leicester, and if on his return to Australia the Tigers are not quite the force they were when he played for them, they are on the way. And they have changed. No doubt a Leicester performance will forever be based on the rigours of sound forward play, but Howard would never have countenanced a side whose only means of attack was the bludgeon.

Leicester will not really know what they have lost until they try to get on without him, but Howard's former assistants Richard Cockerill and Neil Back, holding the fort until Marcelo Loffreda's post-World Cup arrival, have a pretty good idea. For Back, Howard's masterly manipulation and rotation of his squad as the Tigers went through week-by-week games of the highest magnitude last season was equalled only by the extraordinary perceptiveness of his coaching. 'Pat is able to look at a game, analyse it and put it over to the players better than anyone I have experienced,' Back said. 'But at the same time he is the most relaxed, laid-back of men.

'He took a big risk in the way we approached each objective and he had some stick from players about not putting out the best team. But Pat's strength is his ability to treat every game on its own.

'He will look at every opponent, analyse them heavily, decide where their strengths and weaknesses lie and which of our plays are most likely to work against them.'

Coming from an old player of Back's distinction, this is praise indeed.

At Welford Road, Howard worked the trick of being a pal to everyone and no one and retaining a sense of perspective. Here is a man with a degree in pharmacy from the University of Queensland who has other interests in life and so gives rugby its due place. But his beach-bum aura tells only part of the story.

He returned to Leicester in 2004 as John Wells's coaching assistant, and when Wells (now England forwards coach) was whisked away to the less stressful world of the England Academy, Howard agreed to be director of rugby for one season only, 2005-06. Nothing, we were told, would change his mind about then returning to Australia to run a chain of pharmacies he part-owns in Sydney. In the end Leicester persuaded him to stay an extra year, and now he is gone.

It was Simon Cohen, Leicester's operations director, who succeeded in sweet-talking Howard one year, then failed the next. 'Off the pitch he's a shambles,' said Cohen. 'On the pitch he's brilliant. His understanding of the game is quicker than anyone else I've come across. Whatever the weather, it's always sunny in his mind.'

So there was only so much of the English weather he could take, and the tributes that followed him as he made his way back to Australia via a holiday in the Caribbean were as sincere as his own love of Leicester. 'Pat has been phenomenal for us as a player, coach, director of rugby, as a mate,' said Leicester captain Martin Corry, who was arguably better treated at his club by Howard than for

his country by a number of England coaches.

Inevitably the question is already being asked of how long the retiring Howard will stay out of rugby. Can he be serious in his declared intention of pursuing a business career quite divorced from the game? He is steeped in rugby union in a land where it is still more usual to have rugby league as a first sporting love. Howard's grandfather Cyril Towers is credited with the reinvention – or perhaps that should be invention – of Australian back play in the 1920s and 1930s. Howard's father, Jake, was a Wallaby prop in the early 1970s. Howard himself has travelled the world in pursuit of an oval ball, including spending

two years in France with Montferrand. It is a vast sum of knowledge and experience to put to no use.

Bob Dwyer, a World Cup-winning coach who had a less happy experience at Leicester than his young compatriot, has enough admiration to compliment Howard as an 'old-fashioned coach', and, for all his supposed lack of interest, many consider Howard a future Wallaby coach. 'He wants to get out there on the paddock and make players better players,' said Dwyer. 'That type of coach fell out of fashion and a business guy who was well organised was seen as a better proposition.' Which is not to say that Howard, notwithstanding Cohen's remarks about his chaotic lifestyle, is not also well organised as a coach. He could not have taken Leicester to last season's cup and Premiership double otherwise.

While one accepts that plenty of people, including in Leicester itself, would regard the Heineken Cup final defeat as diminishing what had gone before, the way Howard got his Tigers to that point was a strategic and tactical masterpiece. Wasps had been the first club to recognise how the introduction of end-of-season play-offs to determine the

ABOVE Howard of the Brumbies steps inside the Crusaders' Justin Marshall in the final of the 2002 Super 12 competition. Ultimate success eluded Howard on that occasion, the Brumbies going down 34-13 in Christchurch.

LEFT Coach Howard at training in September 2005 with the Tigers' skipper Martin Corry and his fellow back-row forward Lewis Moody.

When it comes to helping drivers after accidents, we're on the ball

"Why not take a look at how we could help you?"

If you've ever been involved in a road accident you'll know how inconvenient it can be...dealing with insurers, repairers, organising a courtesy car...not to mention claiming for any losses or compensation for injury. Even worse when the accident wasn't your fault!

Now there's a better way...simply call Helphire.

We're approved by the UK's leading insurers & can help by:

• Providing you with a like for like vehicle (if needed)
• Organising and funding your repairs
• Liaising with insurers & helping you claim for any losses

The car hire & repair bills are then passed to the insurance company of the driver that caused the accident so you don't have to pay.

You don't have to be a member — just call after an accident that you believe was not your fault and we'll do our best to help you.

Call **0500 224455** or visit **www.helphire.co.uk**

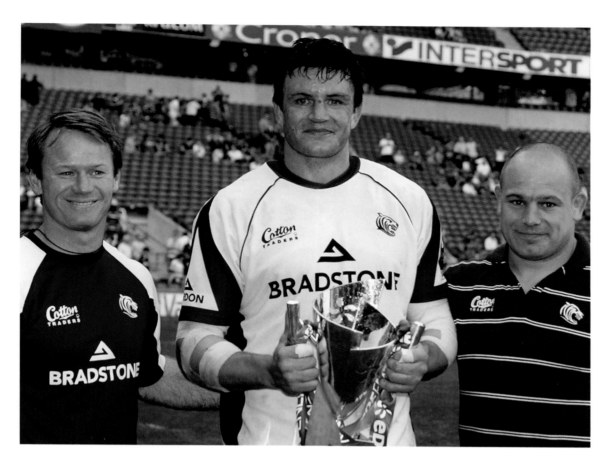

ABOVE A month before sealing the Premiership season by beating Gloucester 44-16 in the play-off final, Howard and his Tigers had come to Twickenham to claim the EDF Energy Cup, defeating the Ospreys 41-35 in the final. Here victorious skipper Martin Corry is flanked by Howard and assistant coach and former Leicester and England hooker Richard Cockerill.

English champions had altered the way in which clubs went through the endurance test of a Premiership campaign. Howard's Leicester followed in planning to reach a peak at the relevant time of the season, the run-in. However abhorrent it may seem, the priority has become not to finish top – which did Gloucester a fat lot of good – but in the top two and have a home semi-final. Failing that, the top four will do reasonably well.

Howard also decided the time had come to expunge the memory of the great players who had seen Leicester through their glory years. Down came the pictures that had been looking down on a group trying to make some more Tigers history. 'We got rid of them all because everyone was still talking about Martin Johnson and that team,' said Cockerill. 'Pat has driven the whole thing. We've worked hard, had our bit of luck and the players have created an ethos of their own.

'At times we left players out not because they had been playing badly but because we wanted to remind them they weren't indispensable. That keeps everyone going because no one is certain of being picked.'

Following that is a fair responsibility for Cockerill, Back and in due course Loffreda. It was typical of Howard that when his end finally came, he 'copped it sweet' and took the blame for Leicester's failure to add the European title to their other two. By then, he knew his players could give no more. 'It's my fault but I'm incredibly proud of what the players have done and what the squad as a whole has accomplished. Credit belongs to them. These players have been absolutely magnificent.'

As he well knows, the feeling is entirely mutual.

The Tigers' Final Push
the 2006-07 Guinness Premiership

by CHRIS JONES

'Dean Ryan, the Gloucester supremo, could only admire the power of the [Leicester] opposition who had left his young backs beaten and bruised'

As Martin Corry raised the Guinness Premiership trophy aloft in front of his delirious Leicester Tigers players and supporters at Twickenham, he had no idea that a week later he would be feeling the same depth of despair just inflicted upon Gloucester. Leicester triumphed 44-16 against a Gloucester team that was, by their own admission, pummelled into the Twickenham turf by a Tigers outfit spearheaded by two-try Alesana Tuilagi. He was too big and too strong for the West Country side. Fast-forward to the following Sunday, and Corry would be reflecting on the Tigers' failure to turn up against London Wasps in the Heineken Cup final. Yes, it probably was the result of too many big games in too short a period, but Corry was still gutted.

By some way, Corry was the English player of the season, having kept his self-belief and form during a dreadful period as England captain in the autumn internationals, then converted into a makeshift second-row for the end of the RBS Six Nations Championship, while all the time driving his Tigers team towards a possible treble. It was a feat no other club had achieved, and at the end of the season Leicester held the Premiership title and the EDF Energy Cup as reward for all that hard work.

Missing out on the Heineken Cup was a severe body blow to a proud club, but it does not diminish the outstanding campaign they enjoyed, one that was – like the Wasps and Sale seasons – shaped by international call-ups and the decision to play Guinness league matches on Test weekends. By the time the Premiership play-off final arrived, Leicester had been robbed by injury of England scrum half Harry Ellis and Italian prop Martin Castrogiovanni.

RIGHT Alesana Tuilagi, Leicester's Samoan wing, streaks away to score his second and his side's fifth try in the Tigers' 44-16 Guinness Premiership final win over Gloucester at Headquarters.

Leicester went into the season with head coach Pat Howard – who would return to Australia once the campaign was completed – insisting they had learnt from Wasps' three Premiership title seasons, which saw the London club become the champions of England without ever finishing the regular season on top. This time it was Leicester who had to be content with second place on points difference behind Gloucester, and they would have been the number one side but for a point deduction for fielding an ineligible player earlier in the season.

In truth, it doesn't really matter whether you finish first or second because you get home advantage, and while Gloucester made that count in abundance against born-again Saracens, the Tigers dealt with Bristol at Welford Road in a match that proved the veterans in the West Country pack still had something left at the end of a very long battle. It wasn't enough to halt Leicester, and when the whistle sounded at the end of the play-off final, it was Leicester who were the champions, and Dean Ryan, the Gloucester supremo, could only admire the power of the opposition who had left his young backs beaten and bruised. 'Today we just couldn't match their power and there's no hiding from that,' said Ryan, who has responded to this fact of life by embarking on a recruitment

drive for next season. 'The whole game is about mismatch and if you've got that across the field ... in reality it was so far across the team it was difficult.

'We were probably stripped of four or five of our most physical players, we've lost physicality across the team. We didn't have the base game that would compete with Leicester. The one thing I'll say is I'm incredibly proud of their achievements over the last few months. This is not the end of the journey for this side, I'm immensely proud of this achievement to get here so early in their progress.'

Corry's post-match reaction was muted because he needed to refocus the players with the European final looming. He said, 'Things went our way, especially the way we finished the first half. We take a huge amount of satisfaction from that. It showed we are dangerous when we have the ball. The most important thing [at half-time] was to carry on playing the way that gave us the lead.'

For much of an absorbing Premiership season the story was dominated by the old men of Bristol, and Richard Hill, their outstanding coach. To the surprise of everyone – including Hill – Bristol were the pacesetters for a good deal of the season, with No. 8 Dan Ward-Smith outstanding and on the way to becoming a key England forward, only for a serious injury to wreck his chances. Men like hooker Mark Regan and lock Roy Winters would be taken to South Africa with England in the summer to prove they were players who could produce the goods at Test level.

Of course, next season asks huge questions of Bristol, who finished third – just as London Irish had done the previous season. The Irish struggled to live up to that mark 12 months later, and the

West Country side – one of seven clubs from England who qualified for the Heineken Cup – will face a similar examination of their ability to evolve.

Hill looked back on his side's season – they went down 26-14 in their semi at Welford Road – with pride, stating, 'It's about getting every ounce out of the players. We've probably achieved right to our maximum. We have planned and prepared carefully, all of us, for every single game. I don't think any point in a game this year has been a fluke. We have had to earn every single point.'

Saracens finished fourth and qualified for the play-off semi-finals despite stumbling to the line. Their performance at Gloucester – a 50-9 defeat – was poor by their own standards and it marked the final appearance in an English club game of full back Thomas Castaignède. He has lit up the Premiership all too infrequently due to various injuries, but when on song he was a joy to watch. His ability to spot a gap and glide past opponents was admired by friend and foe, and he will be missed by the Fez heads.

Sarries' semi-final game at Gloucester was against the backdrop of a Kingsholm ground undergoing major change to highlight the progress being made off the pitch by the top 12 clubs. With attendances increasing, big decisions are being made about future capacities to cater for the new fans who want to be part of the sport. Kick-off times and days are under review, with Newcastle switching back to Sundays from Friday nights to ensure they keep up with the rest of the country.

London Wasps have real problems with their Adams Park base because it needs upgrading to increase capacity and provide better access for fans of the European champions. Wasps finished

fifth, just missing out on the play-offs, and that probably provided the motivation for them to win the Heineken Cup. An intensely proud club, led by that rugby warrior Lawrence Dallaglio, Wasps hated being cast in the unfamiliar role of also-rans. They lost a dozen or so players every time there was a Test match weekend, and this severely undermined their cause. Ian McGeechan pointed out at the end of the season the huge disparity between the team's results when all their players were available and the problems they encountered on Test weekends.

London Irish qualified for Europe at the end of a season that saw Mike Catt fighting a constant battle with injury, and his absence was a contributing factor to their up-and-down challenge. The emergence of Shane Geraghty is a massive plus for the club and England, but they have lost Riki Flutey to Wasps and received Jeremy Staunton in return. It is asking a lot of Staunton to provide the kind of influence and physical impact the New Zealander gave the Irish.

Harlequins started the season with a losing run that suggested they would be going straight back down to the first division. Amid the carnage, Dean Richards, their director of rugby, remained calm. He was absolutely convinced the team would turn things around and he was absolutely right. With young England full back Mike Brown outstanding and Andre Vos making a huge contribution in his final season before returning to South Africa, Quins managed to qualify for the Heineken Cup when Bath failed to win the European Challenge Cup at – ironically – the Twickenham Stoop.

Bath had to be content with an eighth-place finish, which prompted their England lock Steve Borthwick to launch an amazing attack on the club for not showing enough ambition in player recruitment. That is something that could not be levelled at Newcastle, who, with fit-again Jonny Wilkinson, could be a major force next season thanks to the arrival of All Black tight-head prop Carl Hayman. They have brilliant backs and now a man to hold the scrum solid.

For reigning champions Sale, it was one long season of injury problems, which saw Scotland captain Jason White and England No. 10 Charlie Hodgson requiring knee reconstruction surgery. At times, they had to field third- or fourth-choice players in key positions, but amid the wreckage No. 8 Sébastien Chabal stood tall and was still doing his thing for France in New Zealand in the summer. Captain Jason Robinson finished his final season of club rugby with a match-winning try and then needed keyhole surgery after hurting his knee in South Africa – a typical finale for a Sale player at the end of a very cruel season.

In the Wasps' Nest
the 2007 Heineken Cup Final
by ALASTAIR HIGNELL

'Wasps were magnificent. On the biggest stage of all, in front of a world record crowd for a club match, they played some of the best rugby they'd ever played'

I t all seemed too good to be true, and it was. Mills & Boon would have had Leicester's clean-cut hero Pat Howard swaggering off into the rugby sunset with a treble of titles under his belt, along with the record of becoming the first person ever to play in and coach a Heineken Cup-winning side on his CV. But this script was written by McGeechan and Edwards, the star parts were

exclusively reserved for Wasps players, and the affable Aussie could do little but applaud a command performance.

Wasps were magnificent. On the biggest stage of all, in front of a world record crowd for a club match, they played some of the best rugby they'd ever played. An astonishing 80 minutes of power, courage, intelligence and teamwork left an 81,000 crowd begging for more, and a dejected, demoralised Tigers outfit begging for mercy.

No one outside the Wasps camp saw it coming. Leicester, it seemed, had planned their season to perfection. They had already won two Twickenham finals, to lift both the EDF Energy Cup and the Premiership title. Only eight days previously, they had landed the latter with a seven-try, 44-point demolition of Gloucester that demonstrated not just that this generation of Tigers had all the skill, tenacity and cohesiveness of their illustrious predecessors but that they had also

acquired awesome new attacking weapons in the giant shapes of their two South Sea island wings, Seru Rabeni and Alesana Tuilagi.

What's more, the Tigers had form in Europe. Although they had lost their first pool match at home to defending champions Munster, victory in the Thomond Park return had been the defining moment of their season. That success earned the Tigers a home quarter-final – in which they comprehensively outplayed Stade Français – while the draw gave them a Walkers Stadium venue for an even more decisive semi-final dismantling of Llanelli Scarlets.

Wasps had been only slightly less convincing in the Heineken Cup. Emerging as pool winners from a group containing two French teams, they had blown Leinster away at Adams Park in the quarter-finals and were barely extended by Northampton in the semis.

In the Premiership, however, they had – by their own high standards – underperformed. They had failed to win a single match away from home and had suffered telling defeats at the hands of most of the Premiership's basement teams. In their last match of the campaign, which they needed

to win to make the play-offs, they had come up well short against Leicester at Welford Road.

The dominance of Leicester's forwards in that game seemed to presage only doom for Wasps at Twickenham. They had struggled in the set piece all season, and already meagre front-row resources had been stretched even more thinly by long-term injury to England international Tim Payne.

That's where Wasps turned conventional wisdom on its head. Scrummaging coach Craig Dowd – acting on the advice of hooker Raphaël Ibañez and tight-head Phil Vickery – recalled Old Harrovian Tom French from a loan spell at Henley and threw him in against the toughest scrummager in the Premiership, Julian White.

It proved a masterstroke in more ways than one. Not only did the 23-year-old former Wasps Academy player hold his own until the match was nearly done, he also played a key role in the two first-half tries that broke the Tigers' hearts.

With no data available on French, Leicester had no idea where the prop would stand at attacking line outs, or what he would do. When he stepped infield from the front of one such set piece less than 20 minutes into the match, the Tigers believed it was to support his jumper Simon Shaw. Instead, it was to make space for scrum half Eoin Reddan to race onto a short throw from Ibañez, scream past the plodding White and race over the try line unchallenged.

That score gave Wasps the lead for the second time in the match, after an early Alex King penalty had been cancelled out by Andy Goode. The Leicester fly half was to land another two penalties in an immaculate first-half kicking display, but the real damage was done by Wasps' second try.

The Londoners were leading 8-6 at the time, and although they were winning all the key battles in open play, Alex King couldn't make it count on the scoreboard. The fly half's indifferent place-kicking in the first half was to cost Wasps ten missed points. Without that second try they would have been behind at the break.

Bizarrely, and to the lasting horror of Leicester's line-out gurus, it was nearly identical to the first. Yet again the Tigers were caught dozing at the front of the line out. A low, quick throw from Ibañez to Shaw, a return pass from the giant lock and a triumphant gallop to the line from the French hooker once again had red-faced Tigers pounding the Twickenham turf in frustration.

If Ibañez, Shaw and Reddan played their parts to perfection, it was the lesser-known Leon Holden who fed them their lines. The genial line-out expert from New Zealand was rightly given his moment in the spotlight at the post-match media conference. 'I'd studied the tapes of some of their previous matches, and in our Premiership match at Welford Road, I noticed that their line-out support players tended to turn their backs on the thrower on opposition ball. We perfected those moves in the build-up to the final, but I never expected our line-out captain Tom Palmer to call them so early in the game, or so close together.'

If it was Holden's homework that gave Wasps the scent of victory, it was the defensive system perfected by another of their back-room staff that turned it into the heady aroma of triumph. Shaun Edwards had preached throughout the three long, match-free weeks that preceded the Heineken final that the only way to deny Leicester's big bruisers any space or time on the ball was to apply Wasps' trademark blitz defence with even greater ferocity.

Leicester would have known from the team sheet what they were in for. World Cup hero Josh Lewsey was switched to centre in place of the precocious but less physical Dominic Waldouck, and within the first minute he had powered into Leicester's rookie scrum half Frank Murphy. Lewsey's centre partner, Fraser Waters, named man of the match for his organisation of Wasps' defence, was equally implacable. Joe Worsley scythed Leicester players down whenever the opportunity presented itself, Tom Rees won the battle of the open-side flankers against Leicester's Shane Jennings, Lawrence Dallaglio was back to his chest-pumping, jaw-jutting, defiant best and even normally mild-tackling Tom Voyce was inspired not only to halt a rampaging Tuilagi in his tracks but to strip the ball from the giant Samoan for good measure.

And as Wasps tightened their stranglehold on the match, their outside half rediscovered his kicking boots and their replacement back-row forward nearly scored one of Twickenham's great individual tries. James Haskell, on for the tired but magnificent Dallaglio, may have been brought down just short of the Leicester try line after a 70-metre burst, but Alex King confirmed his status as the most decorated No. 10 in the club game with three second-half penalties and a trademark dropped goal as Wasps came home 25-9.

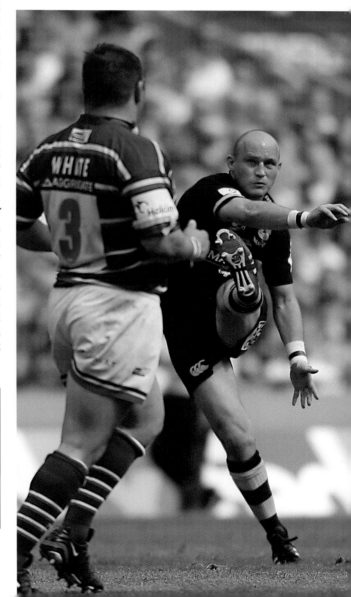

Leicester, so impressive in the run-up to this game, were stopped dead, and failed to come up with a single second-half point. Indeed, the men who had guided them to success in previous months were totally eclipsed. Captain Martin Corry, so inspirational in turning round the Tigers' season, hardly showed at all. Outside half Andy Goode, mastermind of so many of Leicester's previous successes, couldn't come up with a single idea to outwit Wasps' smother defence. Ben Kay and Louis Deacon lost their personal second-row battles against Simon Shaw and Tom Palmer. Leicester, in short, were played off the park as Wasps served up one of the most emphatic Heineken final victories ever. No one could complain. As Pat Howard graciously acknowledged, Leicester were well beaten by the better side on the day. That was the truth and it was good. Very good.

RIGHT Wasps stand-off Alex King drops a 54th-minute goal in front of the Leicester posts.

FACING PAGE Leicester centre Dan Hipkiss tries to round man of the match Fraser Waters.

PAGES 100-01 Captain Lawrence Dallaglio leads the celebrations as Wasps win the Heineken Cup for the second time in four years.

Bath High and Dry
the 2007 Challenge Cup Final

by **TERRY COOPER**

'Their failure to complete a fightback at the Twickenham Stoop when Clermont Auvergne seemed resigned to defeat broke a sequence of six wins for English teams'

If Bath's players had been as articulate with their boots and hands on the pitch as some of them were afterwards in their verbal criticisms of the club's policies, they would surely have managed the converted try they needed for European Challenge Cup final success. Their failure to complete a fightback at the Twickenham Stoop when Clermont Auvergne seemed resigned to defeat broke a sequence of six wins for English teams in this second-tier competition.

England's monopoly comprised triumphs for Wasps and Gloucester and two each for Harlequins and Sale. Defeat cost Bath a place in this season's Heineken Cup and extended a trophy drought that has lasted since the 1998 Heineken Cup final – though they did top the Premiership in 2003-04. And to think that they were the supreme force in the amateur days when they hoovered up ten domestic cups and six leagues. That was part of the point that captain Steve Borthwick was making when he deplored the management's vision. 'Bath have sat on their laurels. Players still come here because of our reputation, but in reality that reputation does not exist any more.'

It might have sounded bad in defeat, but Borthwick made it clear that he would have spoken out, win or lose. He added, 'I hope Bath show some ambition in the summer and invest in a stronger squad. Players are asking why we are not making big signings.'

BELOW Clermont Auvergne captain Aurélien Rougerie is hauled down by Bath's Lee Mears and Steve Borthwick in the European Challenge Cup final at the Twickenham Stoop.

FACING PAGE Clermont wing Julien Malzieu escapes the clutches of Bath full back Nick Abendanon to score his side's first try.

In recent years Bath have released World Cup-winning backs Mike Catt, Mike Tindall and Iain Balshaw and have not replaced them with men of remotely similar quality. Again, Steve Borthwick: 'This group of players are incredibly ambitious and we are pushing the management hard. It should be the other way round. The management needs to support the coaches and players and give us resources – including up-to-date training facilities – so that we can again compete effectively with the best in the Heineken Cup, which we have missed qualifying for once more. Next season we want to achieve big things and qualify for the Heineken, and not finish mid-table and try to rely on this Challenge Cup to scrape into the event where all the major clubs compete. Mid-table is simply not good enough. But until the management's ambition matches that of the players we will be marching uphill.'

And prop David Barnes, speaking with the status of chairman of the Professional Rugby Players' Association, weighed in. 'The Bath "brand" is diminishing year by year. We are losing Andy Williams and Chris Malone right now at the end of this season. There is no sign of reinforcements. Players who can pick and choose are deciding that there are better options than Bath,' lamented Barnes.

His fellow prop David Flatman stated, 'We are blessed in many positions, but there are other positions where players are leaving and have not yet been replaced. David Bory is in tears and leaving the club, but why are we not replacing him with men of the quality of Clermont's wings? We don't want high-profile, famous "rock stars". We want achievement and

results. The loyal players deserve the best. If we get the depth we can beat anybody.'

The final was a slow-burner. Clermont, who finished as runners-up in the 2006-07 French Championship, scored three decisive tries in the second half, having threatened something similar in the opening minutes. Wings Aurélien Rougerie and Julien Malzieu were especially dangerous, making huge tracts of ground. Rougerie was prepared to explore both touch lines, and full back Anthony Floch was positioned for a try but was thrown a forward pass.

Bath needed all their tackling depth. Clermont's Australian stand-off Brock James landed only one of his four penalty attempts – and he was given a hand with his one strike when Barnes upset the referee and the kick was moved many yards forward. Olly Barkley kicked a couple of angled goals for Bath either side of James's effort, but it was not until first-half injury time that Bath entered Clermont's 22 with the ball in hand.

Bath's undeserved lead was put in perspective when Clermont began upholding their reputation as top try scorers back home. They collected three tries between the 5th and 23rd minutes of the second half, though it was a tribute to Bath's scrambling defence that two of them came from kicks behind the defenders, who have a negligible

LEFT Clermont Auvergne fly half Brock James lofts the ball over the oncoming Matt Stevens and Steve Borthwick. An Australian, James has also played for Queensland Reds and Western Force and represented his country in age-grade rugby and at Sevens.

ABOVE Joe Maddock's team-mates rush to congratulate him on his try, which, with Barkley's conversion, put Bath within nine points. They managed only one more penalty, however.

chance if the chips are executed accurately. Disregarding the absence of flanker Sam Broomhall, in the sin-bin spanning half-time, Floch set off on a daring break, which started only 30 yards from his line, then extended it by lobbing a kick over the cover, gathering and feeding Malzieu on the halfway line. The wing easily beat Bory for the opening try.

Hooker Mario Ledesma was the architect of the second. He threw short to a line out, accepted a return pass and almost scored in the corner. The ball was moved across field and scrum half Pierre Mignoni put Tony Marsh in on the blind side of a ruck. Malzieu again shredded Bath's defence with a 60-yard break that James completed with a soft chip that he collected by the posts. James converted twice and hit a post with the other shot.

At 22-6 down, Bath needed something special, and wing Joe Maddock delivered. He was given the ball in apparently heavy traffic 45 yards out. He exploded through it in an unstoppable sidestepping diagonal sprint. Barkley converted. Bath had three close-range line-out opportunities to score in the final 20 minutes. They butchered them all. Substitute Peter Short was rightly adjudged to have lost the ball over the line, and the second line-out chance was wasted when the ball was thrown over the top. Barkley hammered in a 50-yard penalty just before prolonged injury-time started, leaving a six-point gap. The 'last-play' line out gave Bath the ball for over two minutes. They ran through the phases, everybody handled – then Danny Grewcock knocked on. The final whistle went with Clermont 22-16 up.

Borthwick commented, 'It was a huge missed opportunity. We started badly, and we also began our season poorly. We've got to play from the kick-off, otherwise we handicap ourselves. Clermont were there for the taking. We have lost three recent finals and it always hurts.'

Clermont emerged from a group containing Albi, Viadana and Worcester. They beat Newcastle in the quarter-finals and Newport Gwent Dragons in the last four. Bath, for their part, strode past Montpellier, Connacht and Harlequins. They beat Bristol in the quarter-finals and Saracens in the semis. As a postscript to the final, Danny Grewcock was cited for throwing a punch in the match. The ramifications were huge because Grewcock was suspended by European Rugby Cup for six weeks. His ban was timed to end only after England's key World Cup game against South Africa on 14 September. An appeal failed, and he was therefore omitted from coach Brian Ashton's squad.

RIGHT Victorious Clermont Auvergne parade the European Challenge Cup among their travelling fans after the final.

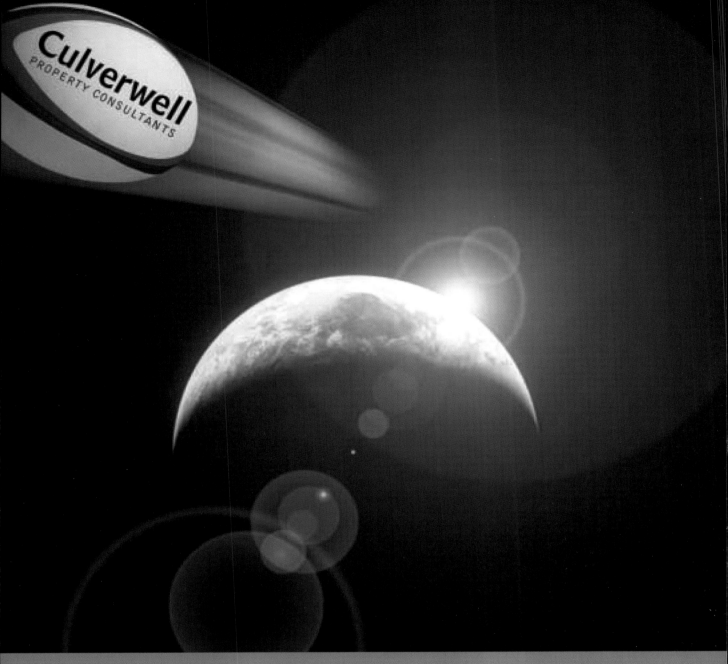

REVIEW OF THE
SEASON 2006-07

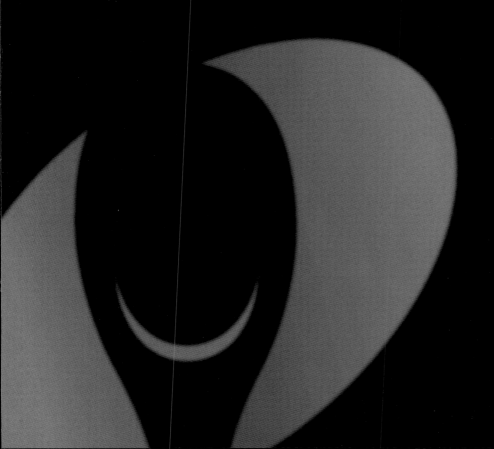

France ... Just the 2007 Six Nations Championship
by CHRIS JONES

'Does even the most bonkers rugby fan really sit down and watch three 90-minute matches – thanks to injury time, that's how long we have these days – in one day?'

Replacement Elvis Vermeulen scored a last-gasp try to give France their fourth RBS Six Nations Championship title in six years. That is a very simplistic way to sum up an extraordinary 2007 tournament that finished in controversy thanks to the decision to allow television to dictate the kick-off times on the last Saturday.

Instead of everyone kicking off at the same time, the games were staggered, which meant France went into their match with Scotland knowing exactly how much points difference they needed to

stop Ireland claiming the title. It all came down to that Vermeulen try, which – ironically – was only awarded after the Irish television match official informed the referee that it was a legitimate score.

The No. 8 barged over from close range deep into injury time to earn the reigning champions a victory by 27 points, three more than they needed to overtake Ireland in the table. While the French celebrated a crucial triumph on home soil just months before they staged the Rugby World Cup, the Irish were left to rue their 'go for broke' tactics against Italy in Rome that allowed their opponents late scores that eventually settled the championship title race.

England could still have won the title if they had beaten Wales by more than 50 points. However, this ludicrous idea was erased from the minds of everyone associated with Brian Ashton's injury-hit team by a deserved Welsh victory in Cardiff that confirmed that while England could win their three home games, they were pretty abject away from Twickenham. The comprehensive defeat at Croke Park in Dublin and that Millennium Stadium setback proved that Ashton still had some way to go to to end England's awful away record.

Kick-off times in the Six Nations tournament have been at the forefront of the debate over the competition's future for some time. Television pays a lot of money and insists on a final 'Mega' Saturday to capture the most impressive ratings figures, but does even the most bonkers rugby fan really sit down and watch three 90-minute matches – thanks to injury time, that's how long we have these days – in one day?

How do you keep the rest of the family from pulling out the plug or hijacking control to try and put something else on the screen? It's a flippant way to address an issue that is not going to go away, with television insisting on another big finale to next season's championship. Past and present players are divided over the issue but accept that a championship should not be won by a team that has a real advantage over its nearest rival just because they are kicking off later.

The Irish were rightly disappointed by the way the title was decided, and on reflection they may have changed tactics in the second half. Instead, they were left to put out a video of their season that was hastily retitled to reflect how close they came without actually becoming the best team in Europe, which much of their play during the championship suggested they were. A last-minute defeat to the French at Croke Park (or 'Choke Park', as they now call it!) was due to wing Vincent Clerc's try, and Irish hopes of a first Grand Slam since 1948 died in an instant.

For France it was a season of much-needed success but also real frustration following their defeat at Twickenham. France were desperate to find a No. 10 who could bring order to some of the chaos that occurs wide out, and David Skrela showed coach Bernard Laporte just how much you need a specialist in that position. The support of Pierre Mignoni, the scrum half, was absolutely vital and he could be the key man for France in the World Cup.

Raphaël Ibañez of Wasps and Sébastien Chabal of Sale proved that Laporte could not ignore those players plying their trades in England. Ibañez, who took over the captain's role from the injured Fabien Pelous, was an inspirational leader and will take his country into the World Cup having worn the armband in 1999 when they were beaten in the final.

BELOW Shane Geraghty makes the break that set up Mike Tindall's try for England against France at Twickenham.

FACING PAGE Kevin Morgan of Wales and Italy's Alessandro Troncon vie for a high ball in Rome in a match that ended amid controversy.

Chabal finally proved the doubters wrong and will be a lock/No. 8 in the World Cup, where his intensely physical play could be a major asset against teams like South Africa and the All Blacks. He started with a barnstorming performance against Italy and caused mayhem in the tournament and on tour in New Zealand months later.

Ireland's eight-try 51-24 victory over Italy in their final Six Nations clash at the Stadio Flaminio in Rome was not enough and they had to be content with another Triple Crown when the players and supporters were desperate for the major prize. There remains a doubt over the Irish team's ability to win a 'big one', particularly the World Cup.

When captain Brian O'Driscoll is fit, Ireland are a potent force, but his early absence left the team looking unbalanced in midfield, particularly against Scotland at Murrayfield. Gordon D'Arcy, to his

immense credit, rose to the challenge of being a new focal point for the team, and his consistency confirmed his arrival as a truly world-class player, giving Ireland two such performers in their midfield.

When Ireland thumped England with a record 43-13 scoreline at their new home at Croke Park, there was a ferocity and clinical approach that suggested O'Driscoll's men were the real deal. As it turned out, the result said more about England, whose home wins over Scotland (42-20), Italy (20-7) and France (26-18) proved they had made Twickenham a fortress again. The defeats on the road confirmed Ashton's problems, and the manner of the 27-18 defeat in Cardiff was very disturbing. Where were the hard-nosed English forwards of old? No wonder they added Lawrence Dallaglio to the World Cup mix, because the team lacked real rugby warriors on the final day of a championship that was supposed to offer the English the chance of becoming the best team in Europe. Rightly they ended up in third place.

At least the championship allowed Jonny Wilkinson to return to England colours after an injury nightmare, and there was one final season of Six Nations rugby for Jason Robinson. Up front, England discovered a real No. 7 in Tom Rees and in the backs, a fleet-footed wing in Dave Strettle to bring a smile to Ashton's face. Harry Ellis became a world-class scrum half but suffered a serious injury that would put him out of the World Cup.

One statistic that highlighted how poor England's pack had become was the lowly 21 turnovers during the five games, which compared very unfavourably with fourth-placed Italy, who managed to steal the opposition ball on 38 occasions. Unfortunately for Italy, a season of great strides forward – including that first ever away win in the championship against the Scots and a home victory against the Welsh – was undermined when coach Pierre Berbizier announced he was leaving.

The former France No. 9 had made Italy a real threat by adding back-line danger to a fearsome pack that can stand toe to toe with anyone and is built around the magnificent Marco Bortolami, their inspirational captain. There was also a recall for veteran scrum half Alessandro Troncon, and he was on great form throughout.

Wales promised much with their brilliant running play – spearheaded by Shane Williams – but lacked the heavy artillery up front until the Welsh forwards found the fire and passion to 'beat up' England in the last match of the season and avoid bottom place. The emergence of James Hook as a world-class No. 10 or centre eased Welsh woes, but it only heaped more pressure on Stephen Jones, the captain and usual outside half.

A wrist injury kept Jones out of the only win over England, allowing Hook to prove he is the real deal and leave Gavin Henson, the former golden boy, with a lot of ground to make up on his Ospreys team-mate. Wales were truly dreadful against Scotland and then found themselves asking the referee if there was time at the death against Italy in Rome to go for the win. He said there was time for a line out and whistled right after it had finished. Cue much gnashing of Welsh teeth and an apology from the official. It was that kind of season for Gareth Jenkins, the Wales coach.

Scotland ended up with the dreaded Wooden Spoon, having failed to cope without injured captain Jason White, who constitutes half their pack. They were unbelievably awful against Italy, playing a wide game that only served to hand the Azzurri interception tries on a regular basis; after less than seven minutes of play, the Scots were 21-0 down. They would have saved themselves but went for tries rather than keeping the scoreboard ticking over and paid the ultimate price, eventually going down 37-17. Only a win over Wales, fashioned by their pack, saved Scotland from a totally disastrous campaign. Not even the return of White is going to make them a real force at the World Cup. The ongoing problems within Scottish rugby with the demise of the Borders side only increased the gloom around the game north of the border. It was a poor return for Chris Paterson, a player who maintained his standards throughout the Six Nations while all those around him struggled to live up to their Test reputations.

The Club Scene
England: The Tigers Resurgent
by BILL MITCHELL

'The club scene produced some highly satisfying moments, notably the fact that all four Heineken Cup semi-finalists were English'

Only the most optimistic and complacent of people will look back on the 2006-07 season with any satisfaction, since the main showcase for rugby in the country – the national team – had few happy moments. As a nation's capabilities and achievements are best judged by its international performances, one should start with a summary of the results at the top level: during the season eleven matches were played, of which four were won and the remainder lost.

In fairness it may be said that the autumn games are usually best used to assess the needs of the squad for the Six Nations campaign, which follows in February and March of the next year. This would suggest that one win in four games was not too bad a return, with the only success at Twickenham being the 23-21 victory over South Africa, who gained revenge the following weekend, winning 25-14. However, a first ever home defeat by Argentina (25-18) was a difficult pill to swallow, even though the Pumas are top-class opposition, and a losing 41-20 scoreline against New Zealand was not encouraging.

The immediate result was that coach Andy Robinson, a thoroughly decent man and really a forwards specialist, had to step down. His replacement, Brian Ashton, made an excellent start by making a gambling selection against Scotland, with Jonny Wilkinson recalled even though his fitness was in doubt. In a 42-20 success, Wilkinson repaid Ashton's faith with his customarily immaculate display of goal-kicking, plus a try, which only the fourth official considered to be genuine. Also superb for England were scrum half Harry Ellis and the experienced former rugby league men, Andy Farrell and Jason Robinson.

Against a greatly improved Italian side, the performance was less satisfactory, although it resulted in a 20-7 victory. Disaster followed in Dublin, where the home country recorded their biggest ever victory in the series (43-13), which might not have been so bad had a certain lock forward, who has been criticised in this column before, not earned himself a ten-minute breather at a vital time, when some decisive points were registered by the Irish.

That error of selection was rectified against France, who arrived at Twickenham as overwhelming favourites and departed well beaten (26-18), thanks to outstanding displays by new cap Toby Flood at fly half, his brief late replacement Shane Geraghty and the swift new wing David Strettle, while the whole pack was excellent. Wilkinson had sustained an injury against the Irish in Dublin and was unfit.

England thus went to Cardiff with an outside chance of winning the championship, but by kick-off time it was clear that France were champions-elect unless the men in white won by an astronomical score at the Millennium Stadium. The opening minute saw the unfortunate Flood have a kick charged down, and the new star man of the Valleys, James Hook, duly scored a try in a match in which inexperience and a lack of discipline led to a 27-18 defeat for England.

If matters had been left to rest there, the bottom line for England might have looked respectable. However, the same error made in 2006 was repeated and a weakened party was sent to South Africa to take on the Springboks at high altitude. Two inevitable thrashings (58-10 and

FACING PAGE Tigers Tom Varndell and Alesana Tuilagi celebrate one of a brace tries for the former in the EDF Energy Cup final win over the Ospreys.

55-22) followed, and the question should be asked: What effect on the morale of young players can such ill-advised ventures have?

Internationally all is not doom and gloom, however. The second-string Saxons won the Churchill Cup at Twickenham with a brave 17-13 final success against New Zealand Maori, while the country's Under 19s managed a creditable sixth place in their World Cup. Nevertheless after several years of fine achievements, the probably underfunded Sevens squad had a poor campaign, which included failure to reach the quarter-finals of both the Twickenham and Murrayfield events.

The club scene produced some highly satisfying moments, notably the fact that all four Heineken Cup semi-finalists were English, with Wasps winning the final most impressively against Leicester (25-9). Bath lost a close European Challenge Cup final against the very good Clermont Auvergne (22-16), although their copybook was blotted by yet another citing for Danny Grewcock, whose six-week suspension may well cause him to miss the World Cup.

England's Premiership saw Gloucester top the table on points difference from Leicester, who duly won the division's 'final' (44-16). Once again the top team went home with nothing, so I make no apologies for suggesting that a trophy should be awarded to the team that has done the hard yards to finish top of the table. Is that too much to ask? It was also sad to report that as high-profile a club as Northampton was relegated from the Premiership, but no team is entitled to special treatment and the Saints are resilient enough to rise again.

In other competitions Leicester won a wonderful Anglo-Welsh (EDF Energy Cup) final against Neath-Swansea Ospreys (41-35) at Twickenham. Cambridge won the Varsity Match (15-6), a result

that might have been different if a brace of crucial passes had not been dropped, while the Army were again Services champions with a 39-25 success against the Royal Navy, both matches also taking place at Twickenham.

The County Championship, which is in effect a competition for junior club players, was won by Devon, who thrashed Lancashire in the final (27-6). The EDF Energy National Trophy went to Cornish Pirates (Penzance & Newlyn), the Intermediate Cup to Mounts Bay, the Senior Vase to Northwich and the Junior Vase to Hartpury College.

So this leaves two unanswered questions. The first of them is: Do England have a chance of retaining the World Cup, given that a team that includes at least seven or eight world-class players will be needed? With the departure of most of the 2003 heroes and doubts about the fitness of Wilkinson and the stamina of the heroic Lawrence Dallaglio, this would seem to be most unlikely, especially with New Zealand looking so superb.

The second of the questions concerns the leading clubs. They have been at war with the RFU for far too long and had threatened to boycott the Heineken Cup, partly because the French clubs felt that it would come too soon after the World Cup. (The English clubs also seem to want a generous subsidy from Headquarters, which does not appear to be forthcoming.) The reasoning failed to take into consideration the fact that the European competitions provide vital income (or at least that appears to be the case to laymen like me), and the only encouraging sign is that common sense may be winning the battle at this juncture. Let us hope so.

Scotland: The Borders Close

by ALAN LORIMER

'The SRU has been grappling with a debt of around £24 million and argued that by ridding itself of the Border Reivers club a rise in this figure could be prevented'

Any reflection on the 2006-07 Scottish club scene should necessarily be bordered in black. For this was the season in which Scotland lost one of its inspirational professional clubs with the untimely axing of the Border Reivers.

The consequence is that Scotland now has only two professional clubs – Glasgow and Edinburgh – to underpin the national team, leaving the elite end of rugby north of the border in a perilous state. The dismantling of the Borders, set up only five years ago, has, too, sparked an exit of top players from Scotland, promoting the thought that Scotland could become like Argentina.

The culling of the Border Reivers has been a bitter blow for an area rightly described as the spiritual heartland of Scottish rugby. Folk in the Scottish Borders, a region in which rugby is everyday chat and where the youth game thrives, are angered by what they see as further evidence that Murrayfield is interested only in the central belt of Scotland.

The reason for the demise of the Borders is all about money. The SRU has been grappling with a debt of around £24 million and argued that by ridding itself of the Border Reivers club a rise in this figure could be prevented. Yet bafflingly SRU chief executive Gordon McKie, who was recruited by Murrayfield to sort out the debt, admitted, 'I don't expect any savings to be made as a result of closing down the Borders'.

Puzzled? So were most observers in Scotland. McKie went on to talk about 'extra investment' in Glasgow and also briefly alluded to 'exit costs'. This latter matter is all about the SRU extricating itself from an agreement made with Gala RFC for use of their ground at Netherdale for professional rugby.

LEFT A wreath and accompanying note laid by Borders fans from Langholm in the middle of the Netherdale pitch at the end of the Reivers' final Magners match against the Ospreys on 12 May.

FACING PAGE Edinburgh Gunners captain Chris Paterson takes on the Leinster defence during the Magners League clash at Murrayfield in September. The Gunners ran out 20-14 winners in this encounter.

That agreement stretched over a 20-year span and bound the SRU into a continuous programme of ground improvement. Netherdale has already benefited and is now the only club ground in Scotland to have undersoil heating, quite apart from having the best playing surface north of the border.

By contrast Glasgow played on what was generally regarded as a substandard ground at Hughenden, in the city's affluent west end. A sale of part of Hughenden to a local builder has meant that Glasgow will decamp to Partick Thistle's stadium at Firhill in the Maryhill area of the city next season. Glasgow may be operating in somewhat depressing conditions, but at least they will have more money to spend. That has allowed coach Sean Lineen to sign up former All Blacks A prop Michael Collins and flying winger Lome Fa'atau. In addition a number of players from the defunct Border Reivers, amongst them Scotland flanker Kelly Brown, have moved to Glasgow.

What is so confusing about the situation in Scotland right now is the question of central ownership. At the outset of professional rugby, the SRU set up four teams, one in each of their regions, with comparative success. Then the powers that be argued for a consolidation and so four became two. After the reality of such a thin base hit home, the then director of rugby, Jim Telfer, argued successfully for a third team to be set up in the Borders. But from the outset, the Netherdale club was hugely underfunded and quickly became the poor relation of Celtic rugby.

When McKie was brought on board to head the SRU's operations at Murrayfield, the axe seemed to hover permanently over the Borders. But there seemed hope of a reprieve when the SRU ceded central control of Edinburgh, in a move that appeared to signal a new direction.

An unofficial 'for sale' sign had gone up, generating a flurry of commercial activity. Yet despite what was allegedly a strong offer to buy Glasgow, the SRU turned down the bid, McKie admitting that they did not want to lose 'central control'. Behind the scenes, however, the sticking point

seemed to be the refusal of the SRU to hand over Heineken Cup and Magners League participation money to any potential buyer.

Just what the exact thinking on professional rugby is within Murrayfield is difficult to fathom. Do they want, as appeared to be the case two years ago, professional rugby to be run by wealthy owners, or do they want to cling on to some control? Right now it is full of contradictions. Yet another idea in the mix is the setting-up of a Magners League 'Scottish' club in London. There have even been suggestions that London Scottish itself be re-formed as a professional club that would, with its academy structure, foster potential Scotland international talent. Meanwhile, the hope at Murrayfield is that the two remaining professional sides north of the border can perform better than last season, when yet again the results were disappointing.

In September and October, all was going well for Edinburgh in the Magners League, but then in the second half of the season international call-ups and the inevitable long list of injuries left the second-stringers struggling against their stronger opponents. Defeats included an embarrassing reverse against Border Reivers. Overall Edinburgh finished mid-table in the league, a far cry from their early promise. Nor did the Heineken Cup provide much more cheer, despite a two-point loss in the opening round to SU Agen and then a one-point win over Leinster. Two defeats by Gloucester sealed Edinburgh's fate.

Fifty miles to the west, Glasgow fared much better in Europe (albeit at a lower level), by reaching the knockout stages of the Challenge Cup, only to lose away to Saracens 23-19 in the quarter-finals. Glasgow also finished ahead of Edinburgh in the Magners League, the Warriors looking strong in the latter part of the season and ending with 11 wins from 20 games.

For Borders, there was the perennial prize of finishing last in the Magners League, an inevitable result of the club's underfunding. Yet as a development tool, the league was invaluable as Borders nurtured the talents of a number of young players this season, among them centre Nick De Luca.

Sadly veteran outside half Gregor Townsend missed much of what was to be his final season, with the result that valuable mentoring was lost.

It was not a whitewash season, however, for Borders. Wins over Leinster and Edinburgh and a number of close games underlined the competitiveness of the Netherdale side, sadly now only a memory for those who backed the concept.

As for the amateur game, and particularly its top end, the cutback in the number of professional teams in Scotland has placed it back in the spotlight. Amateur teams will now have to work with the professional game if their best talent is to be developed properly.

There were signs last season in the streamlined, ten-team Division One that the desired step-up in quality was being obtained. This season, however, the clubs voted for a return to a 12-team format, creating a longer campaign and, it is feared, a dilution of talent.

Last season the ten-team Division One made for a fascinating and continuous competition that was virtually completed before the turn of the year. It produced a first-time championship win for Currie, whose professional approach ensured that the Malleny Park side eclipsed its more fashionable Edinburgh neighbours. At the other end of the table, Aberdeen went down, but two well-known clubs, Stirling County and Edinburgh Academicals, return to the top tier along with GHA.

Currie's title win denied Glasgow Hawks a hat-trick of championship wins, but the Anniesland side atoned in the National Cup competition with what proved to be a comfortable 24-13 win over Edinburgh Academicals at Murrayfield.

For the Division One clubs there was an interesting diversion after the completion of the championship, in the shape of what was termed the Super Cup. This competition was played under the IRB Experimental Law Variations designed to speed up the game. It did, and left players gasping. Mauls allowed to be taken down, handling in the ruck, quick throw-ins – yes, it was indeed a fascinating glimpse of a future direction for rugby union.

Wales: A Good Year for the Regions?
by DAVID STEWART

'To the Ospreys went the headlines. A tired team limped over their final league hurdle at Netherdale ... leaving Lyn Jones's team once again worthy winners'

There is a view that 2006-07 was when the Welsh regional structure, in its fourth season, finally proved its worth. As the Ospreys, Blues and Scarlets finished first, second and fourth respectively in the initial year of the Magners-sponsored Celtic League, the notion has some validity – until one looks at the wider evidence. How effective were the Irish teams last term? Did the Welsh teams perform better than previously in other competitions? And, rather than the structure, is not the depth of local talent and its skill development the key measurement?

To the Ospreys went the headlines. A tired team limped over their final league hurdle at Netherdale 24-16 as the Borders sadly (for the second time) bade farewell to professional rugby, leaving Lyn Jones's team once again worthy winners as they were in 2004-05. And the Ospreys made it to the final of the EDF Energy (Anglo-Welsh) Cup, where they played some terrific rugby in trying to haul back a 28-6 deficit before conceding 41-35 at Twickenham to a Leicester team at the top of its form.

So, why the queries about the coach's longevity? Well, partly because Jones has been in the job for four years plus a lengthy spell at Neath before they and Swansea joined forces – that is about par for a pro coach (the players need to hear a new voice periodically etc); and partly because there is

a nagging suspicion – harsh as it sounds – that with the budget and talent at Jones's disposal, the Ospreys need to move to the next level.

They've yet to make a Heineken quarter-final appearance, although drawing Leicester and Stade Français in recent times is pretty strong mitigation – and they were only a penalty kick away against Sale last term. As an indication of the depth they can call upon, the squad contains the four best Welsh second-rows in Ian Evans, Alun-Wyn Jones, Ian Gough and Brent Cockbain. A friendly draw next time around, and this could be their year. The coach knows expectations are rising, having told his players after Twickenham (in Churchillian mode) that they had reached the end of the beginning. The competitiveness of Justin Marshall will be challenged and complemented by Mike Phillips, serving a back line containing James Hook, Gavin Henson, Sonny Parker, Shane Williams, Nikki Walker and Stefan Terblanche. That represents serious try-scoring potential.

The coaching achievement of the season was undoubtedly that of Paul Turner over at the Dragons in southeast Wales. A man of Gwent, having graced Rodney Parade and the Newbridge Welfare Ground in the 1980s, he's returned from his leafy Home Counties residence to work minor miracles. A squad put together with the sort of transfer wheeler-dealing and talent-spotting that David Jones at Cardiff City would admire plus a team ethic and an effective style of play saw the Dragons overachieve against a backdrop of the smallest budget and poorest facilities in Wales.

With leadership by example from the delightful Kevin Morgan and the cussed old maverick Colin Charvis, a sixth-place finish in the Magners was backed up by the pleasant surprise of a semi-final berth in the European Challenge Cup, in which the Dragons went down 46-29 against the powerful Clermont Auvergne in France. That confidence boost gives Turner something tangible to carry forward, but he'd still welcome a bigger kitty with which to improve the quality of his squad. The loss of Ian Gough – a Newport Gwent man for many years – spoke volumes. Announcing his departure, the front jumper claimed that in forfeiting a testimonial his move west was actually costing him money, before going on to contrast the ambition of his old and new regional outfits.

Cardiff Blues also progressed. A late league run saw them challenge for the title, confounding their many and ongoing critics. The jury that is their long-suffering fans may still be out on the effectiveness of David Young as head coach, but add in the assistance of Rob Howley and the onfield leadership of Xavier Rush and the future may just be a little brighter. Ben Blair was a good capture, and the developing talents of big wing Tom James and second-row Bradley Davies will be closely watched. A better Heineken campaign in a promising pool is a priority. The prodigal Gareth 'Alfie'

Thomas returns from France to add his experience. How much life is left in his well-travelled legs may be open to doubt but not his unique enthusiasm and talismanic qualities.

The return of Phil Davies was the most significant development in the domestic game a year ago. His coaching CV having been forged in the rise, rise and ultimately fall of Leeds, a return to home pastures and picking up the mantle of his mentor Gareth Jenkins was always going to be interesting. At times the Scarlets had become pragmatic, cautious even, towards the end of the Jenkins/Nigel Davies era. Big Phil reacted imaginatively, throwing back the curtains and letting loose the old Stradey style: move it, get there fast, move it again, and if we can do it better and quicker than the opposition, we'll score.

With Llanelli the only Welsh region to seriously target the European theatre, many thought this might be the year the Scarlets emulated their old Munster rivals (who travel to Llanelli again next time around). A perfect six wins out of six in their pool, their thrilling late comeback in Toulouse and a dismantling of Ulster in bad-weathered Ravenhill were the hallmarks of a classy and confident team. Alas the vagaries of the draw meant their semi-final was up at the Walkers Stadium against rampant Leicester, and despite leading after half-time it wasn't to be, the Scarlets going down 33-17. And so the quest for the holy grail continues.

Regan King was probably the best non-Irish centre in the northern hemisphere, and the New Zealanders may yet regret excluding him from their World Cup squad. With the wrongly maligned Stephen Jones and Dwayne Peel, he formed a wily and penetrative axis behind a back row of skill and commitment, spearheaded by Alix Popham and the excellent skipper, Simon Easterby.

It would be churlish not to accept the prevailing view that the regions had their best cumulative outing so far. A mark of further progress next time would be another Magners League title, an EDF Cup win, and someone other than the perennial Scarlets having a really good crack at the Heineken. Stranger things have happened.

LEFT Promising Blues wing Tom James, in action here against the Ospreys in the 2007 EDF Energy Cup semi at the Millennium Stadium, was called up to the Wales squad for the summer tour of Australia.

FACING PAGE Newport Gwent centre Nathan Brew is hauled in by the Clermont Auvergne defence as the Dragons go down fighting 46-29 in the semi-finals of the European Challenge Cup in France. Brew has joined Llanelli Scarlets for 2007-08.

Ireland: Almost But Not Quite

by SEAN DIFFLEY

'And so the season ended with the old Lansdowne Road being demolished … Thomond Park in Limerick and Dublin's Donnybrook ground are also in the hands of the developers'

It was a funny old season, funny peculiar for Ireland's fortunes. There was another Triple Crown success, but somehow that triumph was overshadowed by the failure to manage the Grand Slam. The omens and the bookies were playing up Ireland's chances of a series of wins in the Six Nations and the first Grand Slam since 1948 in the great days of Jack Kyle and company. But while England, Scotland, Wales and Italy were accommodating, the French slipped in a couple of late tries to upset the Irish apple cart. A moment of Irish carelessness in defence at Croke Park provided a typical French opportunity, and France snatched a win against an Ireland team that had dominated and hardly deserved to lose. Then the final moments in Paris. The Irish in Rome had hopefully done enough against Italy, but as they watched TV in their Rome hotel they saw the Grand Slam go to France with that last-gasp try.

A cruel ending, no doubt, but it was still Ireland's best showing for a long time. And then there was the heartening story of Croke Park and the 87,000 crowd standing in the home of Gaelic Games in total respect as, with great emotion, 'God Save the Queen' and the Irish anthems were played. It was an historic moment, and there was the astonishing sight of some mighty players in green shedding a tear or two. In a sense it was so reminiscent of that famous day at Lansdowne Road in 1973, when John Pullin's England team, disdaining threats from terroristic sources, travelled to Dublin to be greeted with that famous prolonged ovation. As they freely admitted, 'We certainly hadn't a hope of winning after that'. Then at the after-match dinner, Pullin brought the house down with 'We may not be very good but at least we turn up!' Indeed, after the 2007 welcome, the England players of 34 years later faced a similar situation as Ireland racked up 43 points for their greatest victory over England.

RIGHT A highly charged moment as the teams line up for the anthems at Croke Park before the Ireland–England Six Nations match.

Overall, the Irish back line was highly impressive, with Brian O'Driscoll and Gordon D'Arcy underlining once again their status as a remarkably talented centre combination and half backs Ronan O'Gara and Peter Stringer providing their expected fine service to their outsides. And of course there was the stellar contribution of lock Paul O'Connell. Next season and in the World Cup, can Ireland continue to cut a dash, despite the problems with sources of back-up in the country's smallish rugby population?

One of the great concerns in the past season was the threat to the Heineken Cup, which is the financial basis of the game in Ireland. Croke Park, with its huge capacity, yielded about £2 million to the IRFU accounts, all badly needed when the cost of the 150 contracted players is about £14 million. The average per professional player is over £80,000, though some, like Brian O'Driscoll, are on big six-figure sums. The total cost of the professional game in Ireland is about £25 million, so it

came as a great relief that the additional sums generated by the Heineken Cup are not now endangered.

But after Munster's success the previous season, the three Irish entries fared less well this past European campaign. There was also much disappointment in the Magners League, the competition that used to be called the Celtic League. Ulster and Munster were poorish, but Leinster flattered only to deceive in the end, being well beaten by Cardiff in the deciding match when they had been well fancied. Leinster's inconsistency is a prime point of discussion in Irish rugby circles, though they were without injured Ireland captain Brian O'Driscoll.

The IRB Under 19 World Championship was staged with considerable success at the Ravenhill ground in Belfast, with full marks to the local fans who thronged to all the matches in a competition won by New Zealand, who beat South Africa in the final. The Irish side performed bravely but were overpowered by the huge opposition, in particular the teams from the southern hemisphere. Charlie McAleese, the Irish coach, referred to that aspect during the tournament. 'What we have to be careful with is that the danger element does not creep in. As the other countries develop in terms of their development, skill, power and physique – you can have the danger element. You can have mismatches as we have seen

ABOVE LEFT Brian Blaney scores a late try in Leinster's 31-0 win over the Borders in the penultimate Magners round of 2006-07.

LEFT Hooker Damien Varley strikes for Garryowen against Cork Constitution in the AIB League Division One final.

FACING PAGE TOP Skipper Paul Neville lifts the Senior Cup. Garryowen beat Belfast Harlequins 20-7 in the final.

FACING PAGE BOTTOM The Seapoint Junior Cup-winning side of 2007.

tonight.' Some of the New Zealand and South African youngsters were as big and as tough-looking as full senior internationals. And to many watching, the thought occurred: 'I wonder how on earth their mothers manage to feed them!'

On the ordinary club front, where amateurism still mainly rules the day, the club of the year was the famed Garryowen. They won the AIB All Ireland League, beating Cork Constitution in the final. Con finished on top of the league, but the system is that the top four then battle it out for the trophy. Garryowen, who had already won the Munster Cup by defeating Con 18-13 in the final, overcame them again, 16-15, in a cracking match; a try just before the end by hooker Damien Varley was converted by out-half Eoghan Hickey. In one of their best seasons, Garryowen also won the All Ireland Senior Cup, beating Belfast Harlequins 20-7 in the final. The Dublin club Seapoint won the All Ireland Junior Cup with a 47-15 final victory over Coleraine.

And so the season ended with the old Lansdowne Road being demolished, to be replaced in about 2009 with a 50,000 all-seated new ground. Thomond Park in Limerick and Dublin's Donnybrook ground are also in the hands of the developers. It's all hands to the JCBs.

France: Saying It With Tries

by CHRIS THAU

'Clermont had lost all their finals, the last in 2001. This was definitely not an encouraging statistical record for the challengers from the south'

Before the semi-finals of the Top 14, *Midi Olympique*, the leading rugby newspaper in France, asked ten Premiership coaches to look into their crystal balls and predict who would be the two finalists. Toulouse got eight votes, Paris five, Biarritz four and Clermont Auvergne one. So much for coaching expertise, though Toulouse, ironically described as 'the Invincibles at half-time', led 12-7 at the break in their semi. Opponents Clermont, on the other hand, produced 80 minutes of sustained, intelligent rugby to counteract Toulouse's forward superiority in front of 55,000 spectators at Stade Vélodrome in Marseilles and ran out 20-15 winners.

BELOW Aurélien Rougerie breaks away from the Toulouse defence during Clermont Auvergne's semi-final win in Marseilles.

FACING PAGE Stade's Brian Liebenberg on his way to score against Biarritz in Bordeaux.

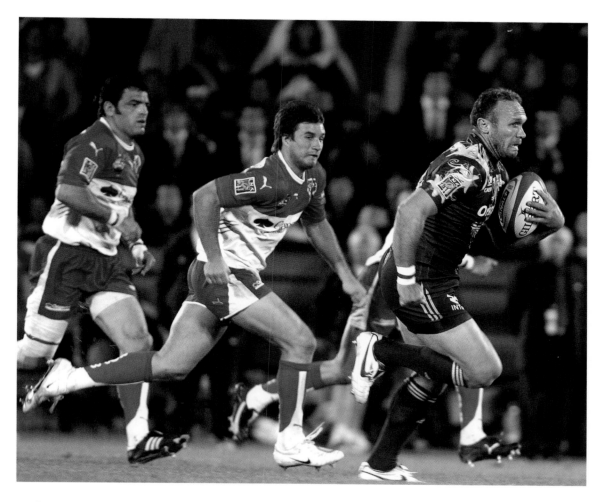

It is difficult to say what acted as an incentive for Clermont's classy performance, though according to club president René Fontès, they played for Edouard Michelin, the former managing partner of Michelin and de facto owner of the club, who drowned during a fishing trip off Brittany the previous year. Whether Clermont Auvergne played for Michelin or not is a moot point; however, they did play for each other like never before, using the try – two signed off by their superstars Tony Marsh and Aurélien Rougerie – to overcome a seemingly tired Toulouse, who had to rely on the boots of Jean-Baptiste Elissalde and Jeff Dubois to put points on the board.

Similarly, in the other semi-final, played in Bordeaux in front of a capacity crowd of 32,000, tries made the difference between the reigning champions Biarritz and Stade Français, the eternal challengers. With Biarritz leading 6-3 at half-time, two Parisian tries in the second half by two of their replacements, giant second-row Radike Samo and centre Brian Liebenberg, put the Parisians in the driving seat, where they remained until the end of the match to win 18-6.

So the 106th championship final for the coveted Bouclier de Brennus brought together Clermont Auvergne, in their eighth final, against Stade Français, in their nineteenth appearance in the last round of the French Championship. Unlike the Parisians, who prior to this match had won the French title 12 times from their previous 18 appearances, Clermont had lost all their finals, the last in 2001. This was definitely not an encouraging statistical record for the challengers from the south.

In repetition of the already familiar pattern established in the semi-finals, with Clermont Auvergne leading 9-0 at half-time through points from the boot, two second-half tries from smiling giant Radike Samo and inspirational captain Agustín Pichot in his last match for the club broke the hearts of the visitors and secured the Parisian team its thirteenth Bouclier in front of 79,000 spectators at the Stade de France. Five penalties from Brock James and one dropped goal from Anthony Floch was all the visitors could muster, while the tries of Pichot and Samo were supplemented by a virtually flawless display of kicking by Argentine superstar Juan Martin Hernández, whose two conversions and three penalties put the nails in the Clermont coffin.

It was an enormous relief for coach Fabien Galthié, who had managed to exorcise the ghosts of the past to win the first Bouclier de Brennus of his coaching career. 'This is because of him and it is for him,' said talisman and captain Pichot when he embraced his coach after the game. Pichot has moved to the other Parisian club, Racing-Métro. Racing, currently in the second professional division, have also managed to sign as head coach one Pierre Berbizier, who will join the club after the Rugby World Cup.

At the other end of the Premiership table, the unthinkable has happened as Narbonne and Agen descended into the boiling cauldron of the second division. Narbonne, suffering from a variety of ills, from unstable management to changes to its playing and coaching personnel, had been sentenced to relegation for some time. Agen, just to add a bit of drama to an already emotionally charged atmosphere, could have escaped had the results elsewhere in the last round as well as the outcome of their match against the champions-to-be Paris been different.

But in the end Albi despatched Narbonne 29-0, Bayonne struggled to overcome Brive 9-6 and Montpellier kept Perpignan within a score, losing 14-9. For the first time after 80 years in the elite of French rugby Agen drop down into a lower division. Hopefully, President Daniel Dubroca will lead the club back into the Premiership as it celebrates its centenary next season.

LEFT Stade Français players with the Bouclier de Brennus in the Champs Elysées the day after their victory over Clermont Auvergne at the Stade de France.

Italy: Green's Swansong

by CHRIS THAU

'The joy of the Treviso players and supporters was dampened soon after the final when Green announced that he was leaving Italy for Australia'

ABOVE Italian Federation president Giancarlo Dondi and the Benetton Treviso team get a good soaking after the Super 10 final against Arix Viadana.

As Benetton Treviso defeated Arix Viadana 28-24 in a hard-fought match in Monza, their coach, Craig Green, who played left wing in the All Blacks' 1987 Rugby World Cup-winning side, strengthened his record as Italy's most successful club coach by picking up a fourth Italian League title in five years. Treviso dominated the early rounds of the Super 10, as the elite section of the Italian League is called, with authority. They finished top of the league, followed by Viadana, Calvisano and Padua – the four clubs that qualified for the knockout stages. Last year's losing finalists, Calvisano, whose sponsor and therefore name changed this year to Cammi Calvisano, got knocked out by their arch-rivals Viadana in the semis – played home and away – while Treviso despatched Carrera Petrarca of Padua, also in the semi-finals, with comparative ease.

In an intense and at times ill-tempered final – referee De Santis showed the yellow card four times – Treviso prevailed through the sheer quality of their game, displaying both style and adventure against a surprisingly competitive Viadana, coached by Green's fellow New Zealander Jim Love. While all Viadana's points came from the boot of Corrado Pilat (seven penalties and a dropped goal), Treviso scored three tries through Franco Sbaraglini, Marco Wentzel and Emiliano Mulieri, with the reliable Marius Goosen adding two conversions and three penalties.

BELOW Incoming Benetton Treviso coach Franco Smith pictured in 2004 during his playing days with the club.

FACING PAGE Pierre Berbizier, who will step down as coach of the Italy national team after the World Cup and for whom a successor has yet to be named.

This was Treviso's thirteenth national title since the club was born as humble Gulf Treviso in 1932. After a period of inactivity during the war, it recommenced as Rugby Treviso in 1945 and won the Italian League title in 1956 for the first time. Once Luciano Benetton became the de facto owner of the club in the 1980s, Benetton Treviso, as it has been called since, never looked back. The club has won ten league titles since 1987, the first in 1989 with Craig Green playing in his customary left wing position.

Green, born in Christchurch in 1961, played for Canterbury under Alex Wyllie and won 20 caps for New Zealand between 1983 and 1987, including the final of the 1987 World Cup, in which tournament he

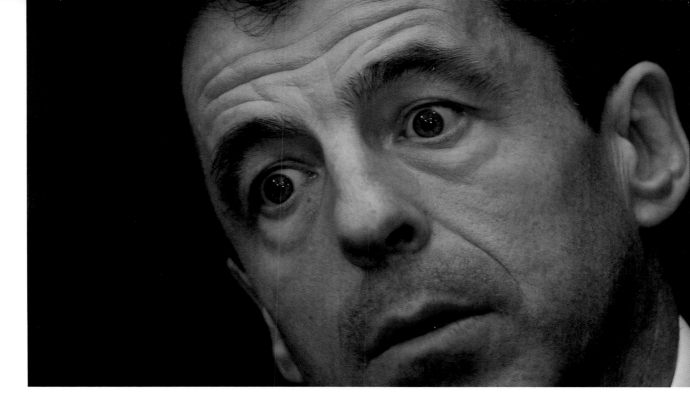

finished as joint top try scorer with John Kirwan. After the World Cup, he came to Italy, where he scored 67 tries in the four seasons he wore the green-and-white jersey of Treviso. Before rejoining Treviso as coach in 2002, Green's coaching CV included a stint as player-coach with Casale, where he ended his playing career; a year in New Zealand with Belfast RFC; a three-year spell with Ghial Amatori & Calvisano; and two years in Japan with Kanto University.

The joy of the Treviso players and supporters was dampened soon after the final when Green announced that he was leaving Italy for Australia. He told the media that he had no immediate plans to get back into coaching Down Under and pointed out, somewhat bitterly, that despite his record he had not been considered for the top Italian coaching job, which will become vacant after RWC 2007. While Benetton Treviso were quick to announce that Green would be replaced by former Springbok fly half Franco Smith, the Italian Federation had been unable to announce a successor to Pierre Berbizier, who declared a few months ago that he was going to leave Italy after the RWC.

Predictably, Berbizier's short reign as head coach of Italy has brought about an upsurge in quality. The 2007 Six Nations was Italy's best international season so far and there are great hopes for a successful RWC campaign and even a place in the last eight. Coaching expertise has become the hallmark of Italian progress, as the quality of the playing personnel goes up season after season. It started with Pierre Villepreux in the 1970s, though progress in terms of quality of outcome and success on the field of play did not come until the 1990s, when French coaches Bertrand Fourcade and Georges Coste were in charge. Coste's diet of teamwork and intensity in preparation paid off spectacularly as Italy came within inches of beating England both in RWC 1995 and in the qualifiers for the 1999 tournament. With the two subsequent New Zealand coaches Brad Johnstone and John Kirwan making a significant contribution to Italy's progress and self-confidence, it was Berbizier's attention to detail and precision that brought about the badly awaited success.

It is said that the Italian president, Giancarlo Dondi, has cast the net far and wide in the search for a successor to Berbizier, with Patrice Lagisquet of Biarritz, Sale's Philippe Saint-André and former Wallaby coach Eddie Jones among the potential candidates. So far, nothing has been decided according to Italian rugby insiders, while it is pointed out that apparently Lagisquet was not prepared to move to Italy, that Saint-André's contract with Sale prevented him moving to a national team other than France and that Eddie Jones was not prepared to commit himself for more than a year. Interestingly enough, the Italian forwards coach, Carlo Orlandi, a former international hooker, who has been deemed good enough to remain in place under both Kirwan and Berbizier, was not considered, allegedly for lack of experience. When does one become experienced in Italian rugby?

A Summary of the Season 2006-07

by TERRY COOPER

INTERNATIONAL RUGBY

NEW ZEALAND TO EUROPE
NOVEMBER 2006

Opponents	Results
ENGLAND	W 41-20
FRANCE	W 47-3
FRANCE	W 23-11
WALES	W 45-10

Played 4 Won 4

AUSTRALIA TO EUROPE
NOVEMBER 2006

Opponents	Results
WALES	D 29-29
ITALY	W 25-18
IRELAND	L 6-21
SCOTLAND	W 44-15

Played 4 Won 2 Drawn 1 Lost 1

SOUTH AFRICA TO IRELAND & ENGLAND
NOVEMBER 2006

Opponents	Results
IRELAND	L 15-32
ENGLAND	L 21-23
ENGLAND	W 25-14

Played 3 Won 1 Lost 2

PACIFIC ISLANDS TO BRITISH ISLES
NOVEMBER 2006

Opponents	Results
WALES	L 20-38
SCOTLAND	L 22-34
IRELAND	L 17-61

Played 3 Lost 3

ARGENTINA TO EUROPE
NOVEMBER 2006

Opponents	Results
ENGLAND	W 25-18
ITALY	W 23-16
FRANCE	L 26-27

Played 3 Won 2 Lost 1

CANADA TO EUROPE
NOVEMBER 2006

Opponents	Results
WALES	L 26-61
ITALY	L 6-41

Played 2 Lost 2

ENGLAND TO SOUTH AFRICA
MAY & JUNE 2007

Opponents	Results
SOUTH AFRICA	L 10-58
SOUTH AFRICA	L 22-55

Played 2 Lost 2

IRELAND TO ARGENTINA
MAY & JUNE 2007

Opponents	Results
ARGENTINA	L 20-22
ARGENTINA	L 0-16

Played 2 Lost 2

WALES TO AUSTRALIA
MAY & JUNE 2007

Opponents	Results
AUSTRALIA	L 23-29
AUSTRALIA	L 0-31

Played 2 Lost 2

FRANCE TO NEW ZEALAND
JUNE 2007

Opponents	Results
NEW ZEALAND	L 11-42
NEW ZEALAND	L 10-61

Played 2 Lost 2

ITALY TO SOUTH AMERICA
JUNE 2007

Opponents	Results
URUGUAY	W 29-5
ARGENTINA	L 6-24

Played 2 Won 1 Lost 1

OTHER INTERNATIONAL MATCHES

Argentina	19	New Zealand	25
Australia	49	Fiji	0
South Africa	35	Samoa	8
Romania	14	France	62
New Zealand	64	Canada	13

ROYAL BANK OF SCOTLAND
SIX NATIONS CHAMPIONSHIP 2007

Results

Italy	3	France	39
England	42	Scotland	20
Wales	9	Ireland	19
England	20	Italy	7
Scotland	21	Wales	9
Ireland	17	France	20
Scotland	17	Italy	37
Ireland	43	England	13
France	32	Wales	21
Scotland	18	Ireland	19
Italy	23	Wales	20
England	26	France	18
Italy	24	Ireland	51
France	46	Scotland	19
Wales	27	England	18

Final Table

	P	W	D	L	F	A	Pts
France	5	4	0	1	155	86	8
Ireland	5	4	0	1	149	84	8
England	5	3	0	2	119	115	6
Italy	5	2	0	3	94	147	4
Wales	5	1	0	4	86	113	2
Scotland	5	1	0	4	95	153	2

UNDER 21 SIX NATIONS

Results

Italy	3	France	42
England	31	Scotland	5
Wales	15	Ireland	17
England	30	Italy	10
Ireland	21	France	16
Scotland	8	Wales	56
France	39	Wales	13
Ireland	13	England	6
Scotland	10	Italy	27
England	13	France	32
Italy	22	Wales	21
Scotland	8	Ireland	31
France	56	Scotland	10
Italy	25	Ireland	36
Wales	21	England	21

Final Table

	P	W	D	L	F	A	Pts
Ireland	5	5	0	0	118	70	10
France	5	4	0	1	185	60	8
England	5	2	1	2	101	81	5
Italy	5	2	0	3	87	139	4
Wales	5	1	1	3	126	107	3
Scotland	5	0	0	5	41	201	0

WOMEN'S SIX NATIONS

Results

England	60	Scotland	0
Wales	10	Ireland	5
Italy	17	France	37
Ireland	10	France	13
England	23	Italy	0
Scotland	0	Wales	10
Scotland	26	Italy	6
France	15	Wales	0
Ireland	0	England	32
Scotland	6	Ireland	18
Italy	0	Wales	24
England	38	France	12
Italy	12	Ireland	17
Wales	0	England	30
France	18	Scotland	10

Final Table

	P	W	D	L	F	A	Pts
England	5	5	0	0	183	12	10
France	5	4	0	1	95	75	8
Wales	5	3	0	2	44	50	6
Ireland	5	2	0	3	50	73	4
Scotland	5	1	0	4	42	112	2
Italy	5	0	0	5	35	127	0

CHURCHILL CUP 2007

(Held in May & June in England)

Pool A

USA	3	England Saxons	51
Scotland A	13	USA	9
England Saxons	18	Scotland A	3

Pool B

Ireland A	39	Canada	20
Canada	23	NZ Maori	59
NZ Maori	50	Ireland A	22

Pool A

	P	W	D	L	BP	Pts
England Saxons	2	2	0	0	1	9
Scotland A	2	1	0	1	0	4
USA	2	0	0	2	1	1

Pool B

	P	W	D	L	BP	Pts
NZ Maori	2	2	0	0	2	10
Ireland A	2	1	0	1	1	5
Canada	2	0	0	2	0	0

Bowl Final

USA	10	Canada	52

Plate Final

Scotland A	21	Ireland A	22

Cup Final

England Saxons	17	NZ Maori	13

Brewed longer for a distinctive, full flavour

Real character doesn t happen overnight.
   Nor are hidden depths immediately obvious.
But given time, they emerge.

WHEN YOU RE READY, YOU LL FIND IT.

UNDER 19 WORLD CHAMPIONSHIP 2007

(Held in April in Northern Ireland)

Eleventh-place Play-off
| Fiji | 60 | Japan | 12 |

Ninth-place Play-off
| Ireland | 34 | Scotland | 0 |

Seventh-place Play-off
| Samoa | 13 | Argentina | 12 |

Fifth-place Play-off
| France | 43 | England | 17 |

Third-place Play-off
| Australia | 25 | Wales | 21 |

Final
| New Zealand | 31 | South Africa | 7 |

UNDER 18 SIX NATIONS FESTIVAL 2007

(Held in April in Scotland)

Results
Scotland	6	England	15
France	16	Wales	30
Italy	5	Ireland	22
England	9	Wales	21
Ireland	8	France	5
Scotland	20	Italy	17
England	23	Ireland	12
Scotland	20	Wales	13
France	34	Italy	7

IRB SEVENS SERIES FINALS 2006-07

Dubai
| South Africa | 31 | New Zealand | 12 |

South Africa (George)
| New Zealand | 24 | South Africa | 17 |

New Zealand (Wellington)
| Samoa | 17 | Fiji | 14 |

United States (San Diego)
| Fiji | 38 | Samoa | 24 |

Hong Kong
| Samoa | 27 | Fiji | 22 |

Australia (Adelaide)
| Fiji | 21 | Samoa | 7 |

England (Twickenham)
| New Zealand | 29 | Fiji | 7 |

Scotland (Murrayfield)
| New Zealand | 34 | Samoa | 5 |

IRB Sevens Champions: New Zealand

IRB PACIFIC NATIONS CUP 2007

Results
Samoa	8	Fiji	3
Australia A	60	Tonga	15
Fiji	30	Japan	15
Samoa	10	Junior All Blacks	31
Fiji	8	Junior All Blacks	57
Tonga	17	Japan	20
Australia A	27	Samoa	15
Tonga	13	Junior All Blacks	39
Australia A	71	Japan	10
Japan	3	Samoa	13
Fiji	15	Tonga	21
Junior All Blacks	50	Australia A	0
Fiji	14	Australia A	14
Samoa	50	Tonga	3
Japan	3	Junior All Blacks	51

Final Table

	P	W	D	L	F	A	BP	Pts
Junior All Blacks	5	5	0	0	228	34	5	25
Australia A	5	3	1	1	172	104	2	16
Samoa	5	3	0	2	96	67	1	13
Fiji	5	1	1	3	70	115	3	9
Tonga	5	1	0	4	69	184	1	5
Japan	5	1	0	4	51	182	0	4

TRI-NATIONS 2007

Results
South Africa	22	Australia	19
South Africa	21	New Zealand	26
Australia	20	New Zealand	15
Australia	25	South Africa	17
New Zealand	33	South Africa	6
New Zealand	26	Australia	12

New Zealand are 2007 Tri-Nations Champions

WE'RE BUILT TO LAST

Travis Perkins

EVERYTHING THE TRADE NEEDS TO GET THE JOB DONE

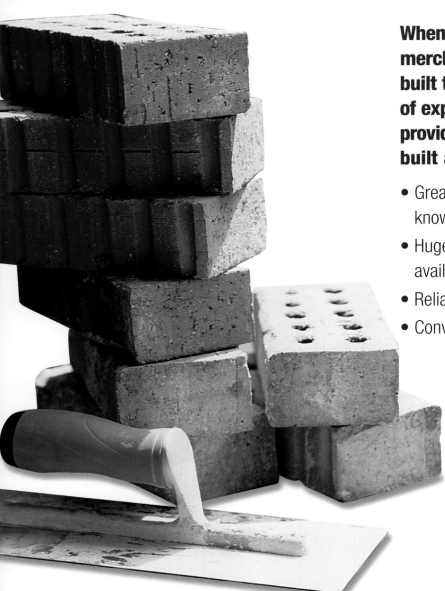

When you choose a builders merchant you want one that's built to last. We've a wealth of experience in the industry, providing a lasting service that's built around your needs including:

- Great service from friendly, knowledgeable staff
- Huge range of building materials available from stock
- Reliable, honest delivery service
- Convenient opening hours

BUILT FOR THE TRADE

www.travisperkins.co.uk

CLUB, COUNTY AND DIVISIONAL RUGBY

ENGLAND (including Anglo-Welsh competitions)

Guinness Premiership

	P	W	D	L	F	A	BP	Pts
Gloucester	22	15	2	5	531	404	7	71
Leicester	22	14	1	7	569	456	14	71*
Bristol	22	14	1	7	398	394	6	64
Saracens	22	12	2	8	539	399	11	63
Wasps	22	12	1	9	504	431	11	61
London Irish	22	12	0	10	398	407	5	53
Harlequins	22	10	0	12	503	438	11	51
Bath	22	8	2	12	428	492	9	45
Newcastle	22	9	0	13	435	528	8	44
Sale	22	8	1	13	414	500	8	42
Worcester	22	6	1	15	346	459	8	34
Northampton	22	6	1	15	342	499	7	33

*Denotes point deducted for fielding an ineligible player

Guinness Premiership Play-offs
Semi-finals

Gloucester	50	Saracens	9
Leicester	26	Bristol	14

Final

Gloucester	16	Leicester	44

National Leagues
Division One Champions: Leeds
Runners-up: Earth Titans
Division Two Champions: Esher
Runners-up: Launceston
Division Three (N) Champions: Blaydon
Runners-up: Tynedale
Division Three (S) Champions: Southend
Runners-up: Westcombe Park

EDF Energy Cup
Semi-finals

Cardiff	10	Ospreys	27
Leicester	29	Sale	19

Final

Leicester	41	Ospreys	35

EDF Energy National Trophy
Quarter-finals

Exeter	43	Lydney	3
Doncaster	10	Penzance/Newlyn	13
Newbury	10	Birm'ham & S'hull	23
Plymouth Albion	17	Coventry	6

Semi-finals

Exeter	19	Birm'ham & S'hull	12
Penzance/Newlyn	17	Plymouth Albion	9

Final

Penzance/Newlyn	19	Exeter	16

EDF Energy Intermediate Cup Final

Dunstablians	35	Mounts Bay	46

EDF Energy Senior Vase Final

Bradford Salem	13	Northwich	18

EDF Energy Junior Vase Final

Hartpury College	72	Billericay	12

County Championship Final (Bill Beaumont Cup)

Devon	27	Lancashire	6

County Championship Shield Final

Warwickshire	22	Somerset	8

County Championship Plate Final

Durham	30	Eastern Counties	20

University Match

Oxford U	6	Cambridge U	15

University U21 Match

Oxford U	14	Cambridge U	12

Women's University Match

Oxford U	37	Cambridge U	7

British Universities Sports Association
Men's Winners: UWE Hartpury
Women's Winners: UWIC

Inter-Services Champions: The Army

Hospitals Cup Winners: GKT

Middlesex Sevens 2006
Winners: Wasps
Runners-up: Leicester

Rosslyn Park Schools Sevens
Festival Winners: King's Taunton
Colts Winners: Whitchurch
Junior Winners: Judd
Preparatory Schools Winners: St Olave's
Girls Schools Winners: Colston's
Open Winners: Colston's

Daily Mail Schools Day
Under 18 Cup Winners: Warwick
Under 18 Vase Winners: Ermysted GS
Under 15 Cup Winners: Lymm HS
Under 15 Vase Winners: Woodhouse Grove

RFUW Women's National Tens: Richmond
Women's Champions: Saracens
Women's Sevens Champions: Richmond

Get laid.

6'3" flat bed. New York from £999 rtn flySILVERJET.com

SCOTLAND

BT Cup Final
Edinburgh Acds	13	Glasgow Hawks	24

BT Shield Final
Garnock	14	Falkirk	15

BT Bowl Final
Morgan Academy FP	18	East Kilbride	11

Scottish Sevens Winners
Kelso: Jed-Forest
Selkirk: Cardiff
Gala: Hawick
Melrose: University of Free State
Berwick: Watsonians
Hawick: Newcastle Falcons
Peebles: Watsonians
Langholm: Newcastle Falcons
Earlston: Selkirk
Jed-Forest: Jed-Forest
Kings of the Sevens: Selkirk

BT Scotland Premiership
Division One

	P	W	D	L	F	A	BP	Pts
Currie	18	14	0	4	566	333	11	67
Ayr	18	12	1	5	390	255	11	61
Watsonians	18	12	0	6	466	325	10	58
Heriot's RC	18	10	0	8	441	353	12	52
Glasgow Hawks	18	10	0	8	414	333	11	51
Boroughmuir	18	7	1	10	464	501	12	42
Melrose	18	9	0	9	357	427	6	42
Dundee HSFP	18	8	0	10	359	424	7	39
Hawick	18	5	0	13	251	450	6	26
Aberdeen GSFP	18	2	0	16	292	599	3	11

Champions: Currie
Relegated: Aberdeen GSFP
Note: For the 2007-08 season there will be a return to 12 clubs in Division One

Division Two

	P	W	D	L	F	A	BP	Pts
Stirling County	22	18	0	4	521	271	10	82
Edinburgh Acds	22	17	0	5	493	345	11	79
GHA	22	15	1	6	455	304	10	72
Jed-Forest	22	11	2	9	349	323	6	54
Hamilton	22	11	0	11	380	366	10	54
Cartha QP	22	8	3	11	382	416	9	47
Stewart's Melville	22	9	0	13	434	469	10	46
Selkirk	22	7	3	12	286	375	7	41
Hillhead/J'hill	22	9	0	13	263	444	5	41
Kelso	22	8	0	14	361	476	8	40
Biggar	22	6	3	13	364	431	9	39
Gala	22	7	0	15	355	423	11	39

Champions: Stirling County
Also promoted: Edinburgh Academicals, GHA
Relegated: Gala
Promoted from Division Three: Haddington, West of Scotland, Musselburgh

WALES

Konica Minolta Cup
Quarter-finals
Aberavon	19	Bridgend	20
Bedwas	14	Llandovery	21
Swansea	8	Cardiff	39
Llanelli	37	Pontypridd	30

Semi-finals
Llandovery	20	Llanelli	19
Cardiff	23	Bridgend	16

Final
Cardiff	18	Llandovery	20

Welsh Premiership
	P	W	D	L	F	A	Pts
Neath	26	17	2	7	704	473	53
Ebbw Vale	26	16	3	7	557	503	51
Newport	26	16	2	8	619	480	50
Pontypridd	26	16	1	9	543	504	49
Llanelli	26	12	2	12	629	509	38
The Wanderers	26	12	2	12	577	602	38
Aberavon	26	12	2	12	603	615	38
Cardiff	26	12	1	13	601	580	37
Swansea	26	12	0	14	487	609	36
Bedwas	26	11	1	14	446	524	34
Bridgend	26	11	0	15	459	508	33
Maesteg	26	10	0	16	531	596	30
Cross Keys	26	9	2	15	485	528	29
Llandovery	26	7	0	19	482	692	21

Welsh Leagues
Division One East
	P	W	D	L	F	A	Pts
Beddau	22	19	0	3	644	309	57
Newbridge	22	17	0	5	516	276	51
Bargoed	22	17	0	5	665	437	51
Pontypool	22	15	0	7	510	368	45
Fleur De Lys	22	10	0	12	410	513	30
UWIC	22	9	1	12	628	604	28
Newport S'cens	22	9	1	12	368	465	28
Llanharan	22	9	0	13	546	555	27
Caerphilly	22	8	0	14	405	575	24
Blackwood	22	6	1	15	433	511	19
Abercynon	22	5	2	15	365	717	17
Ystrad Rhondda	22	5	1	16	410	570	16

Division One West
	P	W	D	L	F	A	Pts
Bonymaen	22	18	0	4	572	296	54
Carmarthen	22	16	0	6	539	297	48
Narberth	22	13	0	9	512	463	39
Bridgend Ath	22	12	1	9	500	446	37
Whitland	22	11	2	9	410	381	35
Merthyr	22	11	0	11	484	421	33
Llangennech	22	10	1	11	474	525	31
Cwmllynfell	22	10	1	11	490	530	31
Dunvant	22	9	0	13	312	419	27
Waunarlwydd	22	6	1	15	390	546	19
Builth Wells	22	6	1	15	340	584	19
Loughor	22	6	1	15	409	524	19

IRELAND

AIB League
Division One

	P	W	D	L	F	A	Pts
Cork Constitution	15	13	1	1	369	227	60
Clontarf	15	10	1	4	325	188	51
Garryowen	15	10	0	5	297	175	48
UL Bohemian	15	10	0	5	306	187	48
Shannon	15	10	1	4	317	200	48
Dungannon	15	7	1	7	261	299	37
Blackrock College	15	6	0	9	348	416	37
Terenure College	15	8	0	7	267	353	36
Lansdowne	15	7	1	7	246	263	33
St Mary's College	15	6	2	7	237	269	32
Galwegians	15	4	2	9	287	324	28
UCD	15	5	1	9	279	372	27
Ballymena	15	4	0	11	265	298	26
Dolphin	15	5	0	10	251	307	26
Belfast H'quins	15	5	0	10	186	266	25
Buccaneers	15	4	2	9	209	306	22

Relegated to Division Two: Belfast Harlequins, Buccaneers

AIB League Play-offs
Semi-finals

Clontarf	15	Garryowen	28
Cork Constitution	21	UL Bohemian	18

Final

Cork Constitution	15	Garryowen	16

Division Two
Champions: Greystones
Runners-up: Old Belvedere

Note: Old Belvedere and Greystones finished the regular season in first and second place respectively in Division Two and were promoted automatically

Division Three
Champions: Bruff
Runners-up: Wanderers

Note: Wanderers and Ballynahinch finished the regular season in first and second place respectively in Division Three and were promoted automatically

Senior Cup Winners
Leinster: Old Belvedere
Munster: Garryowen
Ulster: Dungannon
Connacht: Buccaneers

MAGNERS LEAGUE

	P	W	D	L	F	A	BP	Pts
Ospreys	20	14	0	6	461	374	8	64
Blues	20	13	1	6	447	327	9	63
Leinster	20	12	1	7	472	376	11	61
Scarlets	20	12	0	8	490	417	9	57
Ulster	20	11	1	8	423	310	9	55
Munster	20	12	0	8	379	294	6	54
Glasgow	20	11	0	9	434	419	5	49
Edinburgh	20	8	1	11	335	423	8	42
Dragons	20	8	0	12	353	362	7	39
Connacht	20	4	2	14	326	474	6	26
Borders	20	2	0	18	201	545	4	12

FRANCE

'Top 14' Play-offs

Semi-finals

Stade Français	18	Biarritz	6
Toulouse	15	Clermont Auv'ne	20

Final

Stade Français	23	Clermont Auv'ne	18

ITALY

'Super 10'

Final

Benetton Treviso	28	Arix Viadana	24

NEW ZEALAND

Air New Zealand Cup 2006

Final

Waikato	37	Wellington	31

Ranfurly Shield holders: North Harbour

SOUTH AFRICA

Currie Cup 2006

Final

Free State Cheetahs	28	Blue Bulls	28
(Trophy shared)

HEINEKEN CUP 2007

Quarter-finals

Scarlets	24	Munster	15
Wasps	35	Leinster	13
Biarritz	6	Northampton	7
Leicester	21	Stade Français	20

Semi-finals

Leicester	33	Scarlets	17
Wasps	30	Northampton	13

Final

Leicester	9	Wasps	25

EUROPEAN CHALLENGE CUP 2007

Quarter-finals

Clermont Auvergne	24	Newcastle	19
Bath	51	Bristol	12
Dragons	39	Brive	17
Saracens	23	Glasgow	19

Semi-finals

Clermont Auvergne	46	Dragons	29
Saracens	30	Bath	31

Final

Clermont Auvergne	22	Bath	16

SUPER 14 TOURNAMENT 2007

Final Table

	P	W	D	L	F	A	BP	Pts
Sharks	13	10	0	3	355	214	5	45
Bulls	13	9	0	4	388	223	6	42
Crusaders	13	8	0	5	382	235	10	42
Blues	13	9	0	4	355	235	6	42
Brumbies	13	9	0	4	234	173	4	40
Chiefs	13	7	1	5	373	321	10	40
Western Force	13	6	1	6	276	292	6	32
Hurricanes	13	6	0	7	247	300	3	27
Highlanders	13	5	0	8	235	301	7	27
Stormers	13	6	0	7	249	326	3	27
Cheetahs	13	4	1	8	265	342	4	22
Lions	13	5	0	8	175	284	2	22
Waratahs	13	3	1	9	266	317	7	21
Reds	13	2	0	11	201	438	3	11

Semi-finals

Sharks	34	Blues	18
Bulls	27	Crusaders	12

Final

Sharks	19	Bulls	20

BARBARIANS

Opponents	*Results*
Combined Services	W 33-25
East Midlands	L 21-33
Army	W 14-0
TUNISIA	W 33-10
SPAIN	W 52-26

Played 5 Won 4 Lost 1

PREVIEW OF THE
SEASON 2007-08

Key Players 2007-08

by IAN ROBERTSON

ENGLAND

PHIL VICKERY

Phil Vickery won his first cap for England against Wales in 1998, then went on to play in the World Cup for the first time in 1999 and in all three Tests for the Lions in Australia in 2001. He played a full part in the 2003 World Cup, collecting a winner's medal, and enjoyed a full season in the Six Nations in 2004. He has unfortunately been dogged by a recurring back problem. He has had a series of operations and he seems to be over all his problems and enjoying his rugby once again. Wasps took a calculated risk when they signed him in 2006 after he had played 11 seasons with Gloucester. However, he was restored to full health for the 2007 Six Nations campaign, for which he was made captain, winning his fiftieth cap in February against Scotland. He was rested for England's tour to South Africa in the summer of 2007 but had already been named England captain for the World Cup in France. One of the top props in Europe for the past nine years, he is a great scrummager and can play both loose-head and tight-head. He's athletic in the loose and a good ball player. He is the complete prop.

DAVID STRETTLE

David Strettle had a meteoric rise during the 2006-07 season, emerging from relative anonymity to win his first three full caps for England in the 2007 Six Nations. He began his senior career with Rotherham but switched from Division One rugby to the Guinness Premiership with Harlequins for the start of last season. He had already built up a glowing reputation as a seven-a-side player with England throughout the 2005-06 IRB World Series. His greatest single asset as a Sevens player is his tremendous speed. He is also an elusive runner and he has a natural eye for the gap. His immediate try-scoring success with Harlequins began with a hat-trick against Newcastle. He scored a try for the England Saxons against Ireland A and won his first full cap against Ireland in Dublin. He scored England's only try in that match and went on to play against France and Wales as well. Voted the 2007 Young Player of the Year, he went with England to South Africa in May but suffered food poisoning and was unable to play in either international. Only 24 years of age, he has an exciting career ahead of him.

SCOTLAND

NATHAN HINES

Nathan Hines was born in Wagga Wagga, Australia, and played rugby league for the North Sydney Bears before switching to union with Manly. He moved to Scotland at the age of 24, qualifying to play for Scotland courtesy of his maternal grandfather, who hailed from Govan. No sooner had he arrived than he won his first cap, coming on as a replacement for Scott Murray on the tour of New Zealand in 2000. In fact he came on as a replacement five times in his first seven caps, starting only in the Tests against Canada and the USA. The latter match was a bitter-sweet experience for him – he scored his first try for Scotland and then became the first Scotland player to be sent off in an international. He played for Gala and Edinburgh before moving to France and joining Perpignan. After only a handful of Tests between 2000 and 2003 because of two serious injuries, he bounced back three years ago to firmly establish himself in the Scotland team and has formed a formidable partnership alongside Scott Murray in the second row. At 6ft 7ins and over 18 stones, he is an excellent line-out forward, a strong scrummager and mobile in open play. At last Scotland have a really good line-out presence, with two top-class lock forwards plus the likes of Simon Taylor and Ally Hogg in the back row.

SEAN LAMONT

Sean Lamont began his senior career in England at Rotherham, where he was captain of the Under 21s in 2001. He first sprang to prominence as a member of the Scotland Sevens side at the Commonwealth Games in 2002. The following year he moved from Rotherham to play for Glasgow, where he had a very successful season. He has spent the past three years with Northampton and won his first full cap against Samoa on the Scotland tour in June 2004. Later that year in his first international at Murrayfield, he scored a try against Australia, and the following year he was voted the RBS Man of the Match in the Test against Italy. He is now established in the Scotland side and has become an important and experienced player. He scored two tries against France in Scotland's dramatic victory at Murrayfield in 2006 and so far has seven international tries under his belt. He is immensely powerful, strong in the tackle, quick off the mark and very difficult to stop when in full flight. Scotland need to make full use of his explosive running. The Scottish midfield has been short of experience during the past couple of seasons and has lacked a real cutting edge in attack, but these players can learn from the exploits of Lamont. He involves himself fully in the match, always looking for attacking opportunities, and he should be able to bring out the best in those around him.

WALES

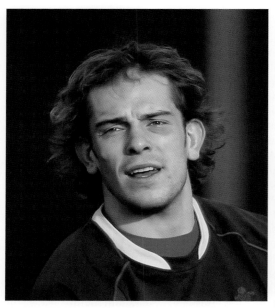

ALUN-WYN JONES

Alun-Wyn Jones began his senior career with Swansea before joining the Ospreys in 2005 and he has been an integral part of the club's forward power for the past three seasons. At 6ft 5ins and over 18 stones, he has rapidly established his credentials as a modern international second-row forward. He is capable of dominating the line out, he is an outstanding scrummager and he is also good in open play. He was named the Principality Premiership Best Newcomer in Welsh Rugby at the end of the 2005-06 season. He began his representative career by playing for Wales Under 21 and he went on to win his first full cap for Wales in June 2006 against Argentina. Initially, he played most of his rugby at blind-side flanker, but he found it easy to adapt to his new role. He had an excellent first full season in international rugby in the 2007 Six Nations. He was particularly impressive against Scotland and he also helped Wales to dominate the line out against the French. In 2005 he enjoyed a particularly successful season helping Wales to an Under 21 Grand Slam. At the tender age of just 22, he is firmly established as one of the best second-rows in international rugby. He is likely to make a significant contribution to the Welsh team over the next few years.

JAMES HOOK

James Hook won his first cap for Wales after a string of outstanding performances for Wales Under 21 as well as playing for the Wales Sevens team in 2005; he scored a match-winning try when Wales beat South Africa in the Plate final at the Commonwealth Games. He joined the Ospreys in September 2006 and received rave reviews for his outstanding performances. He developed surprisingly quickly into a world-class midfield player and he went on to play his first full international for Wales against Argentina under the newly appointed Welsh coach, Gareth Jenkins. He scored a try late in that match, but he had already established himself as a fly half bursting with potential. At the end of his first season in international rugby he was compared favourably to the legendary Barry John, but he was quick to point out that his future was ahead of him and not behind him. He is a gloriously fleet-footed runner with the ball in his hands and he is already acknowledged as a player fully capable of inspiring a whole threequarter line when the occasion demands. He is a multi-talented player who distributes well, is a great kicker of the ball in open play and is also a remarkably accurate goal-kicker. At the end of the 2007 Six Nations Championship Hook was still only 21 years of age, and there is no question he is going to be a major influence in Welsh rugby for many, many years to come.

IRELAND

DAVID WALLACE

David Wallace has enjoyed a distinguished career with both club (Garryowen) and province (Munster). Although he has played occasionally at No. 8, it is as a blind-side flanker that he has established himself and he is one of the greats of Irish rugby in that position. He won his first cap in 2000 against Argentina and had gone on to collect 37 caps by the end of the 2007 Six Nations. He would have won far more had his career not been dogged by three serious long-term injuries. At the start of his international career, he played right through the 2001 Six Nations and was deservedly selected for the 2001 Lions tour to Australia. Part of a remarkable rugby-playing family, his two brothers Paul and Richard also played for Ireland and toured with the Lions. He played throughout the 2002 Six Nations but then because of injury only played nine times for Ireland in the following three and a half years. He re-emerged at his very best in 2006 and is part now of not just a great Irish back row but an excellent Irish pack. At 6ft 2ins and the best part of 16 stones, he is a useful asset at the line out. He is a strong runner and forager, a good ball player and a tremendous tackler. Part of Ireland's recent success has been quite simply that the multi-talented back division are playing behind such a good pack.

BRIAN O'DRISCOLL

O'Driscoll won his first cap for Ireland in 1999 against Australia and went on to play in the World Cup that year; by the end of the 2007 Six Nations, he had won 74 caps for Ireland and been on two Lions tours, in 2001 and 2005. He has become firmly established as one of the greatest centres ever to play for Ireland and indeed is now one of the very best centres in world rugby. Immensely powerful, he is also extremely quick-footed and has a remarkable ability to create half-gaps in the tightest of situations and the strength and blistering acceleration to rip the best-organised defences to shreds. He had not only scored 29 tries for Ireland before the start of the 2007 World Cup but had also shown his versatility by dropping four goals for his country, too. Besides being an exciting runner, he is also one of the great midfield tacklers of his generation. It is no surprise that such a charismatic figure has turned out to be

an outstanding captain of Ireland, leading his team to 20 victories in his first 27 internationals as skipper. He has captained Ireland to two Triple Crowns and he was voted the RBS Player of the Championship in 2007. He led the Lions in New Zealand in 2005 but was unfortunately injured in a dangerous tackle in the opening moments of the first Test; he not only took no further part in the tour but was out of rugby for the next six months. He remains Ireland's most important player.

FRANCE

RAPHAËL IBAÑEZ

Ibañez began his playing career in his home town of Dax and during his time in French Championship rugby he also played for both Perpignan and Castres. He won his first cap for France against Wales in 1996 and has gone on to win more than 70 caps with well over a third of those as captain. He played in back-to-back Grand Slams in 1997 and 1998 and he captained France to the World Cup final against Australia at the Millennium Stadium in Cardiff in 1999. Surprisingly, at the age of just 30, Ibañez retired after the 2003 World Cup to play club rugby in England with Saracens. He was now out of international rugby and not enjoying much success with Saracens. In 2005 he switched to Wasps, who were the top club in the English Premiership, and his career took off once again. He was made captain of France for the whole of the 2007 Six Nations Championship and was inspirational in France finishing top of the table. He rounded off a great season by helping Wasps to win the 2007 Heineken Cup final against Leicester at Twickenham. An outstanding hooker, he is a very accurate thrower-in at the line out and he is dynamic in open play. He is the top international hooker in European rugby and is once again a key member of the French team.

FLORIAN FRITZ

Fritz is one of the talented new players to emerge in French international rugby in the past couple of seasons and was only 21 when he won his first cap against South Africa in 2005. He began his senior career with Bourgoin. After moving to Toulouse he played an influential part in their highly successful Heineken Cup run in 2004-05, which culminated in their beating Stade Français in the final by 18 points to 12. Fritz played in every match in the 2006 Six Nations Championship as well as in the November Test matches at the start of last season. He is a strong, elusive runner with a safe pair of hands and blistering acceleration. He is also an outstanding defensive player. He is one of the very best centres in Europe and the perfect foil for fellow centre Yannick Jauzion. Fritz and Jauzion form one the best centre partnerships in world rugby, with arguably only Brain O'Driscoll and Gordon D'Arcy in the same

league. If France could unearth a top-class fly half they would be almost unstoppable. If Fritz were playing his international rugby outside All Black Daniel Carter, he would surely quickly become one of the great centres of world rugby, but outside the likes of the mercurial Frédéric Michalak or David Skrela life is not quite so straightforward. Nevertheless, Fritz, at the age of 23, is likely to be an influential member of the French team for many years to come.

ITALY

MARCO BORTOLAMI

Marco Bortolami was born in Padua. He began his senior playing career in his home town and began his representative career by captaining the Italy Under 21 side in 2001. Although lock forwards normally reach their peak in their late twenties, so outstanding was he at this level that he won his first full cap that year against Namibia. The following year, he was made captain of the national team at the age of just 22, becoming the youngest captain of Italy ever. He played throughout the 2002 and 2003 seasons and captained Italy in the 2003 World Cup. To further develop his burgeoning career, he switched in 2005 to the French club Narbonne for one season. In 2006 he left France to join Gloucester and played a significant role in their very successful season in the Guinness Premiership, captaining the club. By the end of the 2007 season, he had played 59 times for Italy, captaining 33 times. At 6ft 5ins and over 17 stones, he is a formidable figure in the engine room of the scrum and a commanding player in the line out. He is surprisingly mobile for such a big player, and with his natural footballing ability he has had no difficulty in filling in in the back row when necessary. Still only 27 years of age, he is likely to remain one of the most influential players in the Italian team for the foreseeable future.

ALESSANDRO TRONCON

Alessandro Troncon is one of the most remarkable international rugby players that Italy has produced. He won his first full cap back in the days of amateur rugby in 1994, when he came on as a replacement against Spain. Since that day, he has gone on to play a further 94 Test matches for Italy and is one of a very small group of players to have participated in three World Cups – in South Africa in 1995, Wales in 1999 and Australia in 2003. Barring injury, he is destined to match the amazing record of Jason Leonard by playing in his fourth World Cup in France in 2007. Earlier in his career, before the arrival of Marco Bortolami, he captained Italy in 21 internationals; he also has the proud record of being the most capped player in the history of Italian rugby and looks sure to become the first Italy player to win 100 caps. He has played his club rugby for Benetton Treviso in Italy and also for Clermont Auvergne in

France. About to embark on his fifteenth season in international rugby, he will be remembered partly for his highly successful half-back partnership with fly half Diego Dominguez (they played over 50 Tests together), partly for his try-scoring efforts (16 and still counting) but mainly for his all-round strengths as a top-class scrum half. He has a fast, accurate pass, a strong break in the open, great defensive qualities and he is a hugely competitive player. He is Italy's best back.

Fixtures 2007-08

AUGUST 2007

Sat. 4th	ENGLAND v WALES (WU)
Sat. 11th	ENGLAND v FRANCE (WU)
	SCOTLAND v IRELAND (WU)
Sat. 18th	WALES v ARGENTINA (WU)
	FRANCE v ENGLAND (WU)
Fri. 24th	IRELAND v ITALY (WU)
Sat. 25th	SCOTLAND v S AFRICA (WU)
Sun. 26th	WALES v FRANCE (WU)

SEPTEMBER 2007

Fri. Aug. 31st to	
Sun. Sep. 2nd	Magners League
Sat. 1st	English National Leagues 1-3
	EDF Senior Vase (1)
	EDF Junior Vase (1)
	Scottish Prem/ship 1-3
	Scottish Nat Lges 1-3
	Welsh Principality Premiership
Fri. 7th to	
Sun. 9th	Magners League
Fri. 7th	FRANCE v ARGENTINA (RWC)
Sat. 8th	NEW ZEALAND v ITALY (RWC)
	AUSTRALIA v JAPAN (RWC)
	ENGLAND v USA (RWC)
	English National Leagues 1, 3
	Scottish Prem/ship 1-3
	Scottish Nat Lges 1-3
	Welsh Principality Premiership
Sun. 9th	WALES v CANADA (RWC)
	S AFRICA v SAMOA (RWC)
	SCOTLAND v PORTUGAL (RWC)
	IRELAND v NAMIBIA (RWC)
Tue. 11th	ARGENTINA v GEORGIA (RWC)
Wed. 12th	USA v TONGA (RWC)
	JAPAN v FIJI (RWC)
	ITALY v ROMANIA (RWC)
Fri. 14th to	
Sun. 16th	Guinness English Premiership
Fri. 14th	ENGLAND v S AFRICA (RWC)
Sat. 15th	NZ v PORTUGAL (RWC)
	WALES v AUSTRALIA (RWC)
	IRELAND v GEORGIA (RWC)
	English National Leagues 1-3
	Scottish Prem/ship 1-3
	Scottish Nat Lges 1-3
Sun. 16th	FIJI v CANADA (RWC)
	SAMOA v TONGA (RWC)
	FRANCE v NAMIBIA (RWC)
Tue. 18th	SCOTLAND v ROMANIA (RWC)
Wed. 19th	ITALY v PORTUGAL (RWC)
Thu. 20th	WALES v JAPAN (RWC)
Fri. 21st to	
Sun. 23rd	Guinness English Premiership
	Magners League
Fri. 21st	FRANCE v IRELAND (RWC)
Sat. 22nd	S AFRICA v TONGA (RWC)
	ENGLAND v SAMOA (RWC)
	ARGENTINA v NAMIBIA (RWC)
	English National Leagues 1-3
	EDF Senior Vase (2)
	EDF Junior Vase (2)
	Scottish Prem/ship 1-3
	Scottish Nat Lges 1-3
	Welsh Principality Premiership
Sun. 23th	AUSTRALIA v FIJI (RWC)
	SCOTLAND v NZ (RWC)
Tue. 25th	CANADA v JAPAN (RWC)
	ROMANIA v PORTUGAL (RWC)
Wed. 26th	GEORGIA v NAMIBIA (RWC)
	SAMOA v USA (RWC)
Fri. 28th to	
Sun. 30th	Guinness English Premiership
	Magners League
Fri. 28th	ENGLAND v TONGA (RWC)
Sat. 29th	NZ v ROMANIA (RWC)
	AUSTRALIA v CANADA (RWC)
	WALES v FIJI (RWC)
	SCOTLAND v ITALY (RWC)
	English National Leagues 1-3
	Scottish Prem/ship 1-3
	Scottish Nat Lges 1-3
	Welsh Principality Premiership
	Welsh Konica Minolta Cup (Pr)
Sun. 30th	FRANCE v GEORGIA (RWC)
	IRELAND v ARGENTINA (RWC)
	SOUTH AFRICA v USA (RWC)

OCTOBER 2007

Fri. 5th to	
Sun. 7th	Guinness English Premiership
	Magners League
Sat. 6th	RWC Quarter-finals 1 & 2
	English National Leagues 1-3
	Scottish Prem/ship 1-3
	Scottish Nat Lges 1-3
	AIB Irish Cup (1)
Sun. 7th	RWC Quarter-finals 3 & 4
Fri. 12th to	
Sun. 14th	Guinness English Premiership
	Magners League
Sat. 13th	RWC Semi-final 1
	English National Leagues 1, 2
	EDF National Trophy (1)
	EDF Intermediate Cup (1)
	EDF Senior Vase (3)
	EDF Junior Vase (3)
	Scottish Prem/ship 1-3
	Scottish Nat Lges 1-3
	Welsh Principality Premiership
	AIB Irish Cup (2)
Sun. 14th	RWC Semi-final 2
Fri. 19th to	
Sun. 21st	Guinness English Premiership
Fri. 19th	RWC Third-place Play-off
Sat. 20th	RWC Final (Paris, SdF)

Fri. 26th to	English National Leagues 1-3
Sun. 28th	Scottish Prem/ship 1-3
Sat. 27th	Scottish Nat Lges 1-3
	Welsh Principality Premiership
	Magners League
	EDF Energy Cup (1)
	English National Leagues 1-3
	Scottish Prem/ship 1-3
	Scottish Nat Lges 1-3
	Welsh Principality Premiership
	Welsh Konica Minolta Cup (1)
	AIB Irish Leagues

NOVEMBER 2007

Fri. 2nd to	
Sun. 4th	EDF Energy Cup (2)
	Magners League
Sat. 3rd	English National Leagues 1-3
	Scottish Prem/ship 1-3
	Scottish Nat Lges 1-3
	Welsh Principality Premiership
	AIB Irish Leagues
Fri. 9th to	Heineken Cup (1)
Sun. 11th	European Challenge Cup (1)
Sat. 10th	English National Leagues 1-3
	Scottish Prem/ship 1-3
	Scottish Nat Lges 1-3
	Welsh Principality Premiership
	AIB Irish Leagues
Fri. 16th to	Heineken Cup (2)
Sun. 18th	European Challenge Cup (2)
Sat. 17th	English National League 1
	EDF National Trophy (2)
	EDF Intermediate Cup (2)
	EDF Senior Vase (4)
	EDF Junior Vase (4)
	Scottish Prem/ship 1-3
	Scottish Nat Lges 1-3
	Welsh Principality Premiership
	Welsh Konica Minolta Cup (2)
	AIB Irish Leagues
Fri. 23rd to	
Sun. 25th	Guinness English Premiership
	Magners League
Sat. 24th	English National Leagues 1-3
	Scottish Prem/ship 1-3
	Scottish Nat Lges 1-3

DECEMBER 2007

Fri. Nov. 30th to	
Sun. Dec. 2nd	EDF Energy Cup (3)
	Magners League
Sat. 1st	SOUTH AFRICA v Barbarians
	(Twickenham) (TBC)
	English National Leagues 1-3
	Scottish Prem/ship 1-3
	Scottish Nat Lges 1-3
	Welsh Principality Premiership
	AIB Irish Leagues
Thu. 6th	Oxford U v Cambridge U
	(Twickenham)

Fri. 7th to	Heineken Cup (3)
Sun. 9th	European Challenge Cup (3)
Sat. 8th	English National League 1
	EDF National Trophy (3)
	EDF Intermediate Cup (3)
	EDF Senior Vase (5)
	EDF Junior Vase (5)
	Scottish Prem/ship 1-3
	Scottish Nat Lges 1-3
	Welsh Principality Premiership
	AIB Irish Leagues
Fri. 14th to	Heineken Cup (4)
Sun. 16th	European Challenge Cup (4)
Sat. 15th	English National Leagues 1, 2
	Scottish Prem/ship 1-3
	Scottish Nat Lges 1-3
	Welsh Konica Minolta Cup (3)
	AIB Irish Leagues
Fri. 21st to	
Sun. 23rd	Guinness English Premiership
Fri. 21st	Magners League
Sat. 22nd	English National Leagues 1-3
	Welsh Principality Premiership
Mon. 24th	Scottish National League 1
	(one match)
Wed. 26th	Welsh Principality Premiership
Fri. 28th to	
Sun. 30th	Guinness English Premiership
	Magners League
Sat. 29th	English National League 1
	Welsh Principality Premiership

JANUARY 2008

Tue. 1st	Welsh Principality Premiership
Fri. 4th to	
Sun. 6th	Guinness English Premiership
	Magners League
Sat. 5th	English National Leagues 1-3
	Scottish Prem/ship 1-3
	Scottish Nat Lges 1-3
	Welsh Principality Premiership
	AIB Irish Cup (3)
Fri. 11th to	Heineken Cup (5)
Sun. 13th	European Challenge Cup (5)
Sat. 12th	EDF National Trophy (4)
	EDF Intermediate Cup (4)
	EDF Senior Vase (6)
	EDF Junior Vase (6)
	Scottish Prem/ship 1-3
	Scottish Nat Lges 1-3
	Welsh Principality Premiership
	AIB Irish Leagues
Fri. 18th to	Heineken Cup (6)
Sun. 20th	European Challenge Cup (6)
Sat. 19th	English National Leagues 1-3
	Scottish Prem/ship 1-3
	Scottish Nat Lges 1-3
	Welsh Principality Premiership
	AIB Irish Leagues
Fri. 25th to	
Sun. 27th	Guinness English Premiership
Sat. 26th	English National Leagues 1-3

Scottish Prem/ship 1-3
Scottish Nat Lges 1-3
Welsh Konica Minolta Cup (4)
AIB Irish Leagues

FEBRUARY 2008

Sat. 2nd   IRELAND v ITALY
               (Croke Park, 14:00)
               ENGLAND v WALES
               (Twickenham, 16:30)
               EDF National Trophy (5)
               EDF Intermediate Cup (5)
               EDF Senior Vase (7)
               EDF Junior Vase (7)
               Scottish Cups (1)
               AIB Irish Cup Quarter-finals
Sun. 3rd   SCOTLAND v FRANCE
               (Murrayfield, 15:00)
Fri. 8th   Welsh Principality Premiership
Sat. 9th   WALES v SCOTLAND
               (Millennium S, 14:00)
               FRANCE v IRELAND
               (SdF, 16:00)
               English National Leagues 1-3
Sun. 10th   ITALY v ENGLAND
               (S Flaminio, 14:30)
Fri. 15th to
Sun. 17th   Guinness English Premiership
               Magners League
Sat. 16th   English National Leagues 1-3
               Scottish Cups (2)
               Welsh Konica Minolta Cup (5)
               AIB Irish Leagues
Fri. 22nd to
Sun. 24th   Guinness English Premiership
Sat. 23rd   WALES v ITALY
               (Millennium S, 15:00)
               IRELAND v SCOTLAND
               (Croke Park, 17:00)
               FRANCE v ENGLAND
               (SdF, 20:00)
               English National Leagues 2, 3
               EDF National Trophy Q-finals
               EDF Intermediate Cup Q-finals
               EDF Senior Vase Quarter-finals
               EDF Junior Vase Quarter-finals

MARCH 2008
Fri. Feb. 29th to
Sun. Mar. 2nd Guinness English Premiership
               Magners League
Sat. 1st   English National Leagues 1-3
               Scottish Cups (3)
               Welsh Principality Premiership
               AIB Irish Leagues
Fri. 7th to
Sun.9th   Guinness English Premiership
Sat. 8th   IRELAND v WALES
               (Croke Park, 13:15)
               SCOTLAND v ENGLAND
               (Murrayfield, 15:15)
               English National Leagues 1,3

Sun. 9th   AIB Irish Cup Semi-finals
               FRANCE v ITALY
               (SdF, 15:00)
Fri. 14th to
Sun. 16th   Guinness English Premiership
Fri. 14th   Welsh Principality Premiership
Sat. 15th   ITALY v SCOTLAND
               (S Flaminio, 13:00)
               ENGLAND v IRELAND
               (Twickenham, 15:00)
               WALES v FRANCE
               (Millennium S, 17:00)
               English National Leagues 2, 3
               EDF National Trophy Semi-finals
               EDF Intermediate Cup S-finals
               EDF Senior Vase Semi-finals
               EDF Junior Vase Semi-finals
               Scottish Cups (4)
Fri. 21st to
Sun. 23rd   Guinness English Premiership
               Magners League
Sat. 22nd   EDF Energy Cup Semi-finals
               English National League 1
               Scottish Prem/ship 1-3
               Scottish Nat Lges 1-3
               Welsh Principality Premiership
               AIB Irish Leagues
Fri. 28th to
Sun. 30th   Guinness English Premiership
               Magners League
Sat. 29th   English National Leagues 1-3
               Scottish Prem/ship 1-3
               Scottish Nat Lges 1-3
               Welsh Principality Premiership
               Welsh Konica Minolta Cup Q-fs
               AIB Irish Leagues

APRIL 2008
Fri. 4th to   Heineken Cup Quarter-finals
Sun. 6th   European Challenge Cup Q-fs
Sat. 5th   English National League 1
               Scottish Cups (5)
               Welsh Principality Premiership
Fri. 11th to
Sun. 13th   Guinness English Premiership
               Magners League
Sat. 12th   EDF Energy Cup Final
               English National Leagues 2, 3
               EDF National Trophy Final
               EDF Intermediate Cup Final
               EDF Senior Vase Final
               EDF Junior Vase Final
               Welsh Principality Premiership
               AIB Irish Cup Final
Fri. 18th to
Sun. 20th   Guinness English Premiership
               Magners League
Sat. 19th   English National Leagues 1-3
               Scottish Cups (6)
               Welsh Principality Premiership
               Welsh Konica Minolta Cup S-fs
               AIB Irish Leagues

Fri. 25th to Sun. 27th Sat. 26th	Heineken Cup Semi-finals European Challenge Cup S-fs English National Leagues 1, 2 English National 3 Play-off County Championship Plate (1) Welsh Principality Premiership

MAY 2008

Fri. 2nd to Sun. 4th	Guinness English Premiership Magners League
Sat. 3rd	County Championship 　　　(Bill Beaumont Cup, 1) County Championship Shield (1) County Championship Plate (2) Scottish Cups Finals AIB Irish Leagues Semi-finals
Fri. 9th to Sun. 11th	Guinness English Premiership Magners League
Sat. 10th	County Championship 　　　(Bill Beaumont Cup, 2) County Championship Shield (2) County Championship Plate (3) Nat U20s Champ/ship S-finals Welsh Konica Minolta Cup Final AIB Irish Leagues Final
Fri. 16th to Sun. 18th	Guinness English Premiership 　　　(Semi-finals)
Sat. 17th	County Championship 　　　(Bill Beaumont Cup, 3) County Championship Shield (3) County Championship Plate S-fs
Fri. 23rd to Sun. 25th Sat. 24th	Heineken Cup Final European Challenge Cup Final County Championship 　　　(Bill Beaumont Cup, Final) County Ch/ship Shield Final County Ch/ship Plate Final Nat U20s Championship Final
Sat. 31st	Guinness English Premiership 　　　(Final)

Rugby's charity supporting disadvantaged children and young people

Mission Statement

Wooden Spoon aims to enhance the quality and
prospect of life for children and young persons in the
United Kingdom who are presently disadvantaged either
physically, mentally or socially

Charity Registration No: 326691

THE SPORTING CLUB

PROUD SUPPORTERS OF WOODEN SPOON

"GOOD FOOD IN A RELAXING ATMOSPHERE, WITH SUPERB AFTER DINNER SPEAKERS"

Now in its seventeenth year, the Sporting Club successfully administrates Clubs in nine areas of the Midlands, West Country and London. The principal objective of Sporting Club Dinners is to provide members with the environment in which to entertain clients, colleagues or friends in pleasant surroundings with excellent speakers from the World of Sport.

The Clubs	Venues
Capital	The London Marriott, Grosvenor Square
East Midlands	East Midlands Conference Centre
Gloucestershire	Thistle Hotel, Cheltenham
North Worcestershire	Worcester Rugby Club
Solihull	The Renaissance Hotel, Solihull
South Staffordshire	The Molineux, Wolverhampton F C
South Warwickshire	Warwick Hilton, Warwick
Sutton Coldfield	Moor Hall Hotel & Spa
West Country	Marriott Hotel, Bristol

Previous speakers have included:-

Sports	Sporting Speakers
Rugby	Jason Leonard OBE, Gareth Edwards, Will Greenwood MBE
Cricket	Shane Warne, Dickie Bird MBE, Ian Botham OBE
Snooker	Steve Davis OBE, John Parrott MBE, Denis Taylor
Football	Sir Geoff Hurst, Jack Charlton OBE, Matt Le Tissier
Boxing	Sir Henry Cooper, Alan Minter, Frank Bruno
Others	Sir Stirling Moss, Sir Ranulph Fiennes, Roger Black MBE

If you wish to attend a Sporting Club Dinner please contact
David Trick
Telephone: 01373 830720   Facsimile: 01373 830999
Email - david@sportingclubgroup.com
Or Visit www.sportingclubgroup.com for further details

The Sporting Club (UK) Ltd, P O Box 3582, Laverton, Bath, BA2 7ZR